THE VIOLENT EARTH

STORM

JENNY WOOD

Wayland

Titles in this series

Earthquake
Flood
Storm
Volcano

Series Editor: Sarah Doughty
Designer: Tony Truscott
Artist: Nick Hawken
Consultant: The Meteorological
Office, Bracknell

First published in 1992 by
Wayland (Publishers) Ltd
61 Western Road, Hove
East Sussex, BN3 1JD, England

British Library Cataloguing in
Publication Data
Wood, Jenny
 Storm. – (Violent Earth series)
 I. Title II. Series
 551.56

HARDBACK ISBN 0-7502-0410-9

PAPERBACK ISBN 0-7502-1336-1

Typeset by Tony Truscott Designs
Printed in Italy by Rotolito Lombarda S.p.A.

Picture: Storm clouds darken the sky over
Sidmouth Beach in Devon, England.

CONTENTS

Disaster!	4
What is a storm?	6
A look at weather	8
Thunderstorms	10
Snowstorms	12
Dust storms and sandstorms	14
Tornadoes	16
Hurricanes	20
Storm-hit countries	22
Prediction and control	26
Projects	28
Glossary	30
Books to read	31
Index	32

DISASTER!

The storm hits

On 10 November 1970, meteorologists noticed a tropical storm or cyclone developing in the Bay of Bengal, off the coast of East Pakistan (now Bangladesh). On 13 November, the storm hit. Violent winds sweeping over the ocean had whipped up a huge tidal wave which surged over the flat, low-lying land. A newspaper report described how, '...the tidal wave, as high as a two-storey building, has changed the map of the delta, sweeping away islands and making others. Whole communities have been destroyed and all their people and livestock killed.'

Survivors of the 1970 cyclone search for personal belongings in what is left of their homes.

The coast of Bangladesh, showing the area which suffered the most severe flooding and the greatest damage during the 1970 cyclone.

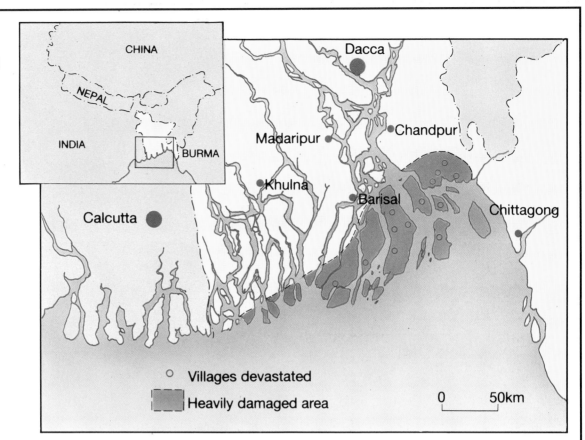

CHINA
NEPAL
INDIA
BURMA
Dacca
Madaripur
Chandpur
Khulna
Barisal
Calcutta
Chittagong

○ Villages devastated

Heavily damaged area

0   50km

Tidal wave kills 150,000

The death toll
At the time, the death toll was thought to be 150,000. But the storm hit at harvest time, when there were many extra workers in the area, and many of those who survived the storm itself may have died later from hunger or from diseases such as dysentery and typhoid. It is possible, therefore, that as many as one million people may have died – about one-sixth of the area's entire population.

The after effects
An international aid effort began immediately. British and American planes flew into the capital, Dacca, carrying vehicles and helicopters as well as food and medical supplies. The vehicles and helicopters were used to transport the food and medical supplies to the areas which had been cut off completely by the floodwaters. The British Royal Navy also sent two ships to Dacca, to act as a central base from where the supply of aid could be co-ordinated.

The flat land of Bangladesh has no natural barriers to keep out the sea, and it has been hit by many more natural disasters in recent years.

WHAT IS A STORM?

Huge, grey-black clouds gather on the horizon. Slowly they roll across the sky. Suddenly, the sky glows as a flash of lightning bursts through the darkness. Seconds later, the air echoes with the angry rumbling of thunder. Finally, the rain starts to fall.

Heavy rain, thunder and lightning are what most people think of when they are asked to describe a storm. A storm is a period of very bad, sometimes violent weather and may consist of rain, thunder, lightning, hail, snow, strong winds, or any mixture of these.

The storm's damage

Storms occur over both land and sea. Some affect only a small area and last for only a few hours. Others, driven by fierce winds, move across a much wider area and last for days or even weeks. The most severe storms can affect a whole country, sometimes even a whole continent.

Storms can be devastating in their effects. In November 1966, for example, the city of Florence in northern Italy received one-third of its usual annual rainfall in two days. The river Arno, which flows through Florence, burst its banks and muddy flood waters poured through the streets. As well as causing chaos in towns, heavy rain can also

damage fields of crops in the countryside.

In very cold conditions, rain turns into snow. Snowstorms can block roads and railway lines, and make it impossible for people to move around. Strong winds can uproot trees and bring down electricity cables and telephone lines. Some winds are so powerful that they can flatten buildings and destroy whole towns. During the very worst storms, many people are killed.

A summer storm over Tucson, Arizona, USA. Bright flashes of lightning illuminate the night sky.

A LOOK AT WEATHER

Weather is the state or condition of the air in the troposphere (the lowest level of the atmosphere) at a particular time. But the condition of the air is constantly changing, and so the weather changes too, from hot to cold, dry to wet and calm to windy.

Changes in the weather

Weather changes occur, first of all, because the temperature of the air changes. As the Sun's rays warm the surface of the Earth, heat is released into the troposphere. This heat, in turn, warms up the air around it.

Moisture released into the troposphere returns to the Earth in the form of rain, hail and snow.

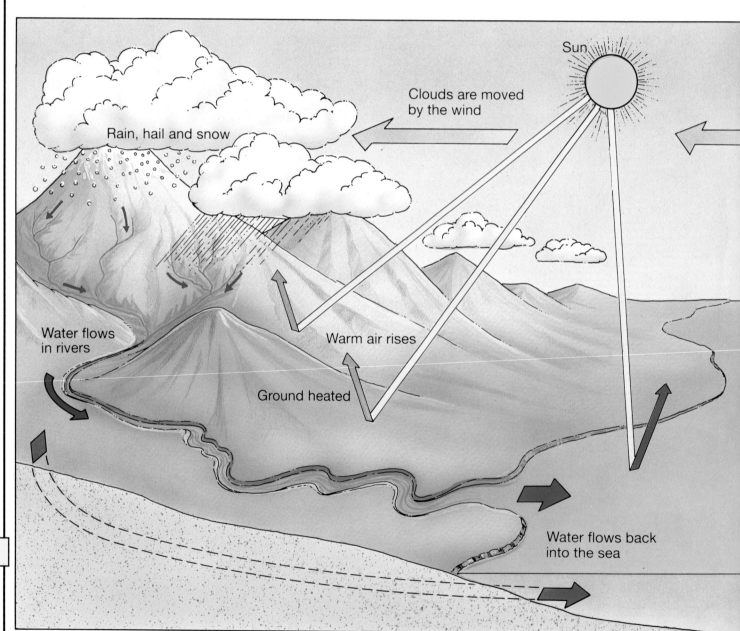

Sun

Clouds are moved by the wind

Rain, hail and snow

Warm air rises

Ground heated

Water flows in rivers

Water flows back into the sea

When a cold air mass meets a warm air mass, a depression forms and storms occur. The main diagram shows a cross-section of the area marked A – B on the inset.

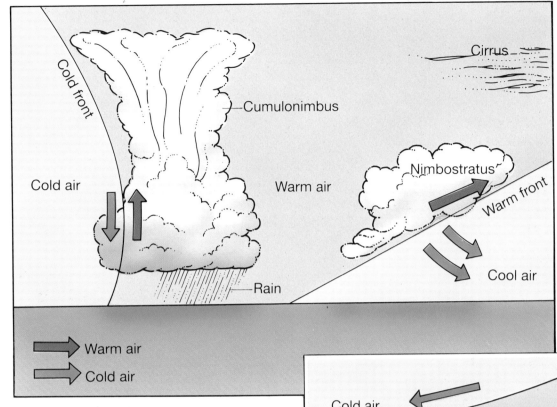

Cold front

Cumulonimbus

Cirrus

Cold air

Warm air

Nimbostratus

Warm front

Cool air

Rain

→ Warm air

→ Cold air

Moisture in the air forms clouds

Water evaporates from the sea

But warm air rises and, as the warm air drifts upwards, cold air sweeps in to take its place. So large masses of warm and cold air constantly jostle for position, creating winds and changes in temperature.

The amount of moisture in the air affects the weather too. The Sun's rays cause moisture to be released from seas and rivers into the troposphere. Air can hold a certain amount of moisture but when it reaches its limit, any extra moisture condenses into water droplets, and clouds form. These water droplets may eventually fall as rain, hail or snow. Warm air can hold more moisture than cold air, so if the air is cold, rain, hail or snow are more likely to occur.

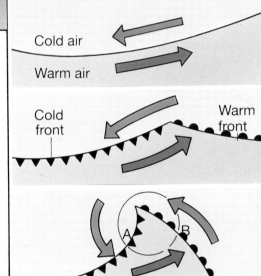

Cold air

Warm air

Cold front

Warm front

A

B

How storms occur
Storms occur when cold and warm air masses meet. The air masses do not mix and clouds form along the edge or 'front'. The greater the difference in temperature between the two air masses, and the larger the air masses are, the more violent the storms are likely to be.

THUNDERSTORMS

At any time, about 1,800 thunderstorms are happening throughout the world. Thunderstorms are the most common type of storm.

They usually occur when the air is warm and damp. As the warm air rises, it cools down and the moisture it contains forms clouds.

Lightning occurs when negative electrical charges flow towards positive charges, or vice versa.

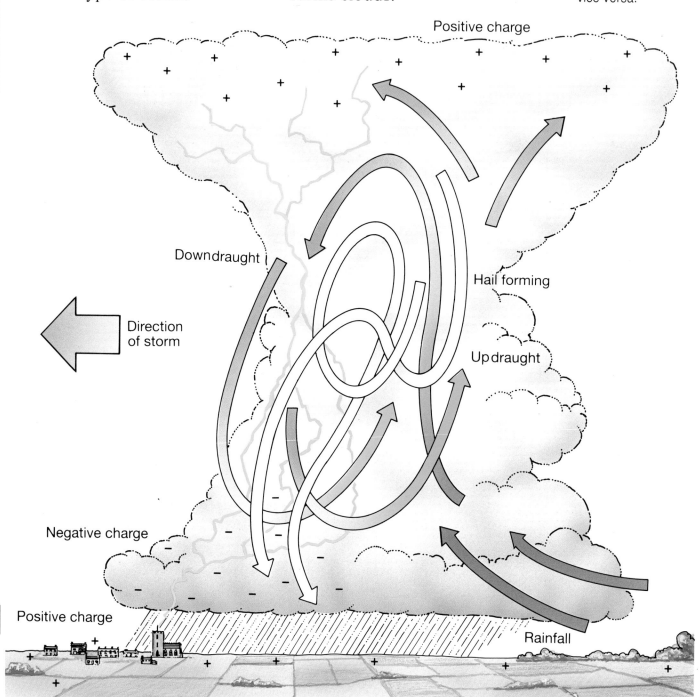

Positive charge

Downdraught

Hail forming

Direction of storm

Updraught

Negative charge

Positive charge

Rainfall

A thundercloud producing very heavy rainfall in Australia. Rainstorms may cover only a small area, but can cause severe flooding.

Thunderclouds

The clouds which build up to produce thunderstorms are called cumulonimbus. They are huge, grey-black clouds which can stretch so high into the atmosphere that the water droplets in the tops of the clouds turn into ice crystals. Sometimes these ice crystals melt, and form raindrops. But sometimes the crystals remain frozen, and eventually fall as hailstones.

Lightning

Inside a cumulonimbus cloud, fast-moving currents of air rise and fall, tossing the water droplets and ice crystals around violently. This furious movement causes electric charges to build up within the cloud. Eventually, these charges become so strong that the electricity is released in the form of a giant spark which we know as lightning.

Thunder

Lightning heats the air in its path to over 33,000°C – five times hotter than the surface of the Sun! The heated air expands quickly. As it does so, it collides with the surrounding cool air. This collision of hot and cold air produces sound-waves that we hear as thunder.

Thunder and lightning always occur together, at exactly the same time. But because light travels faster than sound, we always see lightning before we hear thunder. The amount of time between a flash of lightning and a clap of thunder tells you how far away the thunderstorm is. Every five seconds counts as a distance of 2 km.

SNOWSTORMS

A fall of snow can look beautiful, but as little as 10 cm of snow lying on the ground is enough to cause chaos. Snow can block roads, bring down telephone lines and electricity cables and maroon people in their homes.

> '...the manner in which snow often arrives in a blizzard, or departs by avalanche or thaw flood, means that snow must be considered a treacherous enemy.' (I. Holford, author of a book on British weather.)

The cause of snowstorms

Snowstorms occur when a mass of freezing air moves out from the polar regions. When it meets a mass of warm air, the warm air rises quickly, causing a heavy snowstorm. Snow falls from a cloud only if the temperature of the air between the base of the cloud and the ground is below 4°C. If the temperature is higher, the snowflakes will melt as they travel through the air and fall as rain or sleet.

When icy polar air meets a warm air mass, the cold air undercuts the warm air ahead. A huge bank of clouds forms, bringing heavy snow showers.

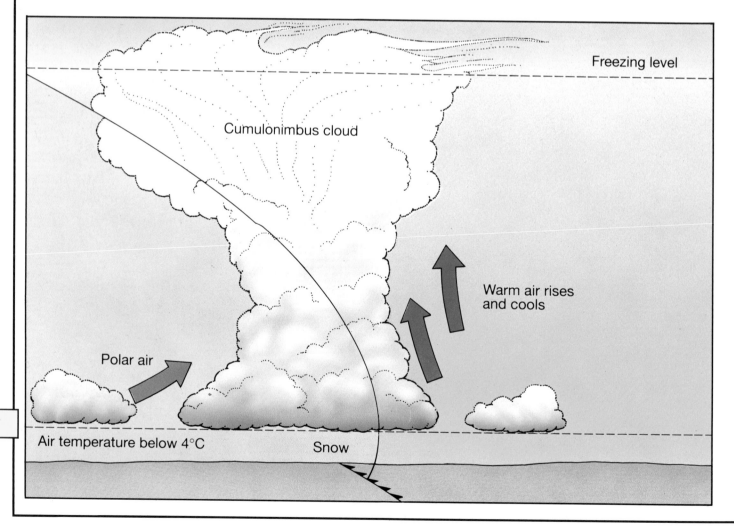

Freezing level

Cumulonimbus cloud

Warm air rises and cools

Polar air

Air temperature below 4°C

Snow

Although all snowflakes have six sides, they vary in shape and size. One snowflake may consist of as many as 100 ice crystals and be over 2.5 cm in diameter.

A snowplough is being used to clear snow from roads after a heavy snowstorm in the USA.

The formation of snowflakes

Snowflakes are produced by ice crystals in a cloud colliding and sticking together. All snowflakes have six sides, but of all the billions of snowflakes which have fallen on the earth, it seems that no two are exactly alike. The different shapes reflect the different weather conditions in which they are produced. Needle and rod shapes form in very cold air. More complicated patterns form in warmer air.

Blizzards

The worst kind of snowstorm is called a blizzard. During a blizzard, strong winds blow the snow into huge piles called snowdrifts, which can bury farm animals and cars, and prevent people moving out of their homes for days at a time. It is dangerous to travel during a blizzard, as the air temperature may be as low as –12°C, and visibility less than 150 m.

DUST STORMS AND SANDSTORMS

Dust storms

Dust storms occur in places where the soil is very dry and has no vegetation to protect it. Fierce winds blow across the land, lifting the dry, dusty soil high into the air and carrying it away. After a severe dust storm, it may be impossible to grow crops on the land for a number of years.

Below: An American family, affected by the terrible 'Dust Bowl' droughts of the 1930s, pray for rain.

'When the night came again it was black night, for the stars could not pierce the dust to get down, and the window lights could not even spread beyond their own yards. Now the dust was evenly mixed with the air... Houses were shut tight, and cloths wedged around doors and windows... In the morning the dust hung like fog, and the sun was as red as ripe new blood.' (A passage from 'The Grapes of Wrath' by John Steinbeck.)

The Dust Bowl

By the early 1900s, many people had settled in the Midwestern states of the USA and begun to farm the fertile land. Soon, the area became one of the world's largest wheat-growing areas, and was nicknamed 'the bread basket of America'.

At the beginning of the 1930s, heatwaves and drought began to dry up the soil. Then, in 1934, came the first great dust storm. Fierce winds whipped up the

Travellers struggling across the desert during a sandstorm in Cameroon, West Africa.

loose top layer of soil and carried over 300 million tonnes of dirt all the way to the east coast. The dust storms continued, over forty of them occurring in 1935 alone. It became impossible to farm the land, now known as the Dust Bowl, and thousands of bankrupt farmers and their families had no choice but to move west towards California in search of whatever work they could find.

Sandstorms

Most sandstorms occur in dry, desert areas. Strong winds whisk up the top, loose layer of sand and carry it through the air. The swirling sand forms a low cloud about 50 cm above the ground. The sand moves erratically, as the grains collide with each other. Sandstorms are dangerous to desert travellers because they cannot find their way. Sandstorms can also damage crops and clog up machinery.

A tornado is a type of violent whirlwind. This whirlwind is a column of air that spins across an area of land at tremendous speed, causing terrible damage. Tornadoes are usually accompanied by heavy rain, thunder and lightning. Most tornadoes occur in the Midwestern and Southern states of the USA.

How a tornado forms
A tornado forms over land when a mass of cool, dry air collides with a mass of warm, damp air coming from the opposite direction. Cumulonimbus clouds form along the front or 'squall line' where the two air masses meet. The warm air rises very quickly. As it does so, more warm air rushes in to take its place. This air also rises, and begins to rotate in the base of the cloud. The rotating air then spirals downwards from the cloud, in the shape of a funnel. A hissing sound can be heard as the funnel moves towards the earth. If the funnel reaches the ground, it raises a cloud of dust and debris. The hissing becomes a roar. Then the tornado whirls across the land, sweeping up objects and destroying almost everything in its path.

A tornado's speed
Most tornadoes travel over an area of about 30 km, at speeds of between 15 and 40 kph. But some travel ten times that distance, at speeds of up to 100 kph. The speed of the winds whirling around the centre of the storm is difficult to measure, because the tornado usually destroys everything in sight, including instruments set up to record its progress, but the figure may be in the region of 600 kph.

The distinctive funnel cloud of a tornado spirals towards the ground.

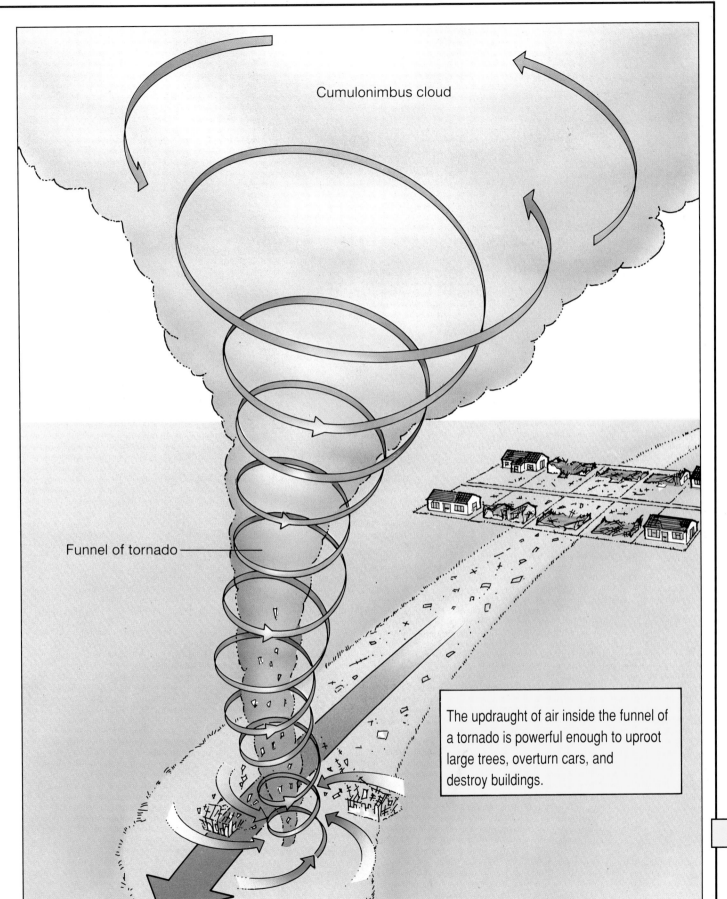

Cumulonimbus cloud

Funnel of tornado

The updraught of air inside the funnel of a tornado is powerful enough to uproot large trees, overturn cars, and destroy buildings.

About 700 tornadoes or 'twisters' as they are frequently called, are reported each year in the USA. Most occur in spring, in the afternoon or evening of a hot, humid day.

Advance warning

Scientists of the National Weather Service constantly gather reports from weather stations all over the USA. If a tornado is likely to develop, the Service broadcasts this information on television and radio. When a tornado is spotted, the Service issues a warning to all the communities likely to lie in the tornado's path. The inhabitants of many tornado-hit areas have learnt over the years where to take cover. Some have even built special underground storm cellars in which to shelter until the danger is past.

The devastating after-effects of a tornado on a town in Illinois, USA.

'...bark has been peeled off trees, harnesses have been stripped off horses, and clothing has been stripped off people leaving them completely naked. Dead sheep have been found shorn of their wool, feathers have been plucked off chickens...' (An American expert describing the sucking effect of a tornado.)

18

Disaster strikes!

On 2 and 3 April 1974, more than 100 tornadoes roared across a vast area of the USA from Alabama and Georgia in the south, through Ohio and Kentucky further north, right across the Canadian border into Ontario. Many of the areas lay outside the usual tornado belt, and so were unused to such fierce storms.

In a period of eight hours, over 300 people were killed and hundreds more injured. Damage to property was estimated at hundreds of millions of dollars. Three-quarters of the buildings in a town in Kentucky were demolished. In Ohio, the top floor of the high school was blown away. Guin, a small town in Alabama, completely disappeared. 'Guin just isn't there,' said a state trooper when the storm damage became apparent.

HURRICANES

Like a tornado, a hurricane is a powerful, whirling windstorm. But hurricanes form over warm ocean water, not over land. Hurricanes are much larger than tornadoes, and can measure as much as 480 km in diameter. A hurricane may last for several hours, sometimes days, and can travel a great distance across the ocean and over land. Hurricanes that form over the Pacific Ocean are often called typhoons or cyclones.

Formation of hurricanes

Hurricanes develop over the warm seas on either side of the Equator, at times when the air is warm and moist, and the temperature is over 26°C. As the sea heats the air, a current of warm, moist air rises above the water. Winds rush in below this air current and whirl upwards. As they rise, they cool, and the huge amounts of water vapour they contain form towering storm clouds. At the centre of a hurricane is a calm area known as the eye. Surrounding the eye are 'wall clouds' where the strongest winds (up to 240 kph) and heaviest rain occur.

The path of a hurricane

As a hurricane moves over the ocean, it stirs up huge waves on the surface of the sea.

If these waves reach land, they cause immense damage, flooding towns and cities, and killing many people.

When a hurricane moves over land, strong winds and heavy rain batter the area for several hours and may cause devastation. Then, as the eye passes over the area, there is a brief period of calm until the winds on the other side of the hurricane arrive, causing more destruction.

A hurricane needs warm, moist air from the sea to give it energy. As the hurricane moves over land, it begins to die down very gradually.

Right: This photograph, taken over the Gulf of Mexico in August 1980, shows clearly the circular shape of a hurricane and the eye at the centre of the storm.

Below: The air in the eye of a hurricane does not rise although it is warmer than the air in the rest of the storm. Instead, the air sinks downwards.

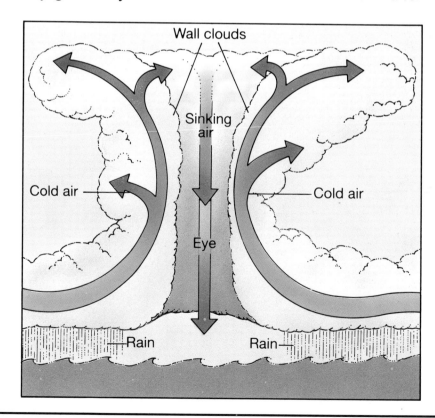

20

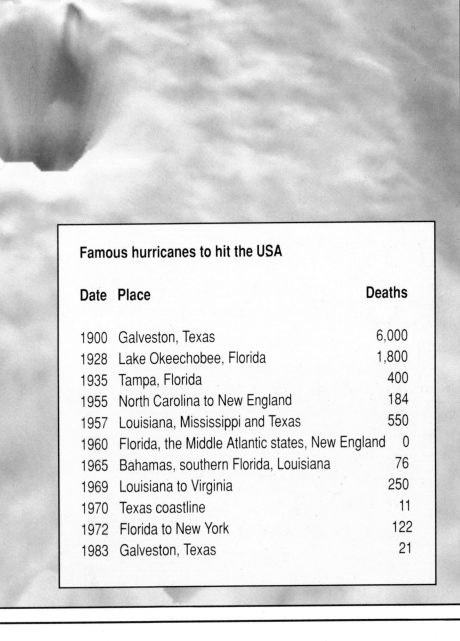

Famous hurricanes to hit the USA

Date	Place	Deaths
1900	Galveston, Texas	6,000
1928	Lake Okeechobee, Florida	1,800
1935	Tampa, Florida	400
1955	North Carolina to New England	184
1957	Louisiana, Mississippi and Texas	550
1960	Florida, the Middle Atlantic states, New England	0
1965	Bahamas, southern Florida, Louisiana	76
1969	Louisiana to Virginia	250
1970	Texas coastline	11
1972	Florida to New York	122
1983	Galveston, Texas	21

Many areas of the world are regularly hit by severe storms, often with devastating effects.

The USA
The USA, the world's fourth largest country, suffers heavy rainstorms, snowstorms, hurricanes, tornadoes and dust storms, all causing terrible damage and loss of life. The Midwestern and Southern states are frequently hit by tornadoes, while areas near the Atlantic Ocean and the Gulf of Mexico are affected by hurricanes.

Buildings and land still suffer terrible storm damage but advance warning systems in the USA now save many people's lives.

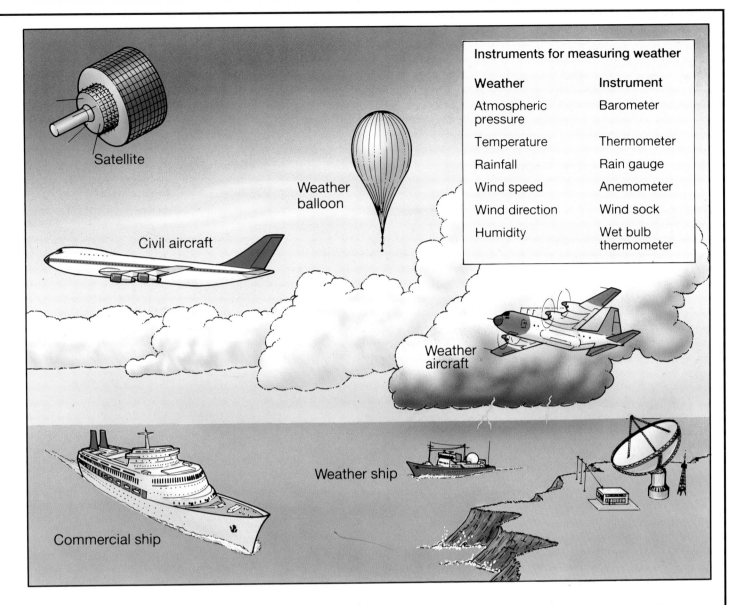

Instruments for measuring weather

Weather	Instrument
Atmospheric pressure	Barometer
Temperature	Thermometer
Rainfall	Rain gauge
Wind speed	Anemometer
Wind direction	Wind sock
Humidity	Wet bulb thermometer

Satellite

Weather balloon

Civil aircraft

Weather aircraft

Weather ship

Commercial ship

This diagram shows some of the ways that weather forecasters gather information and collect data about the condition of the atmosphere.

The area around the Great Lakes, and the state of New England often receive such heavy snowfalls that the land is covered in snow for between 90 and 140 days each year.

Warning in advance
In many ways, however, the people of the USA are fortunate. Storm-warning systems are now highly efficient. Meteorologists examine photographs taken by weather satellites, and collect information on wind speeds and temperature. The data collected can warn them of bad weather so people are frequently able to flee an area before a storm strikes. Many people have their own transport, too, which makes evacuation easier. Some can afford to build storm shelters, and architects have developed ways of strengthening buildings to withstand storm damage. The numbers of deaths associated with natural disasters has decreased steadily in the USA over the last 50 years.

Developing countries

Poorer countries are not so fortunate. In places such as Bangladesh, the Philippines and Taiwan, even if storm warnings are given well in advance, most people just have to sit tight and hope that they will survive. Few have their own transport, and houses are often built of wood or other natural materials which cannot withstand the force of a tropical storm. Many of these countries are low-lying, while others are islands, and so they have little or no protection against the power of a storm-swept sea. Death tolls are often huge, and the survivors often find it impossible to scratch a living from the devastated land.

Hurricane Fifi

On 18 September 1974, the Central American country of Honduras was hit by Hurricane Fifi. The hurricane arrived in the middle of the night, sweeping away homes, roads, bridges and railway tracks. The torrential rain caused rivers to flood. In the city of San Pedro Sula, 400,000 people were left homeless and without food.

Before the hurricane struck, Honduras was a poor country, struggling for survival. Its economy depended on its two main exports, bananas and coffee. Both crops were completely destroyed. The country's food crops were destroyed, too, and many people

Satellite photographs are used to monitor the development of tropical storms. But it is not always possible for people to escape before the storm arrives.

Survivors of Hurricane Fifi amongst the ruins of their home.

starved to death. Overseas aid was provided but the effects of the hurricane on such a poor country were terrible and long-lasting.

Meteorologists in Canada gathering information on temperature and wind speed.

Weather forecasting is important in many ways to all sorts of people. Facts and figures about the weather are recorded constantly by weather stations all around the world.

This information is sent to meteorologists in weather forecasting centres, who use computers to help them analyse the information. The computers print out maps which show how weather conditions are likely to change over the following days and weeks.

Weather forecasting equipment
As well as using computers, meteorologists now have many sophisticated instruments to help them find out about the weather. Weather satellites are able to take photographs of Earth from high up in the atmosphere. These photographs provide valuable information about the progress of storms. Meteorologists use radar, too, to help them make more accurate weather forecasts. Radar pictures can show the position of rain, snow and hail. An experienced forecaster can use this information to make weather predictions.

Controlling the weather
It is very unlikely that scientists will ever be able to control the weather, but they are experimenting with ways of altering weather conditions on a small scale. One of these ways is called cloud seeding. Chemicals

are sprayed or dropped into clouds to trigger off rainfall. Cloud seeding is most often used to produce rain over very dry areas, but it can also be used to reduce the strength of a storm. This includes lessening the possible damage caused by lighting and heavy hailstones. As rainfall is released from the cloud, the storm's energy fades.

Advance warning
Perhaps the most important achievement in weather forecasting to date is the ability of meteorologists to give accurate advance warning of storms. Disasters do still occur, but predictions of hurricanes, tornadoes and floods have, on many occasions, saved thousands of lives.

Computers help meteorologists make accurate predictions about the weather.

1.Making an electric charge

Lightning is caused by static electricity. Electric charges build up in the air until they are discharged. A flash of lightning is a huge discharge of electricity. You can make static electricity by rubbing together a comb and a piece of woollen or nylon cloth. When the comb is charged with static electricity, it can pull at things rather like a magnet does. This is why pieces of paper become attached to the comb. Once they are attached, the pull stops, and eventually the paper falls off. This means the electric charge has gone.

Materials:
A comb
A piece of paper
Scissors
A piece of woollen or nylon cloth

Method:

1. Cut the sheet of paper into small pieces.

2. Rub the cloth with the comb, using strong, quick movements.

3. Hold the comb near the pieces of paper. What happens?

Another way of demonstrating static electricity is by rubbing a comb on a woollen jumper then holding it near a friend's hair. Watch what happens. Some of the hair should rise up towards the comb.

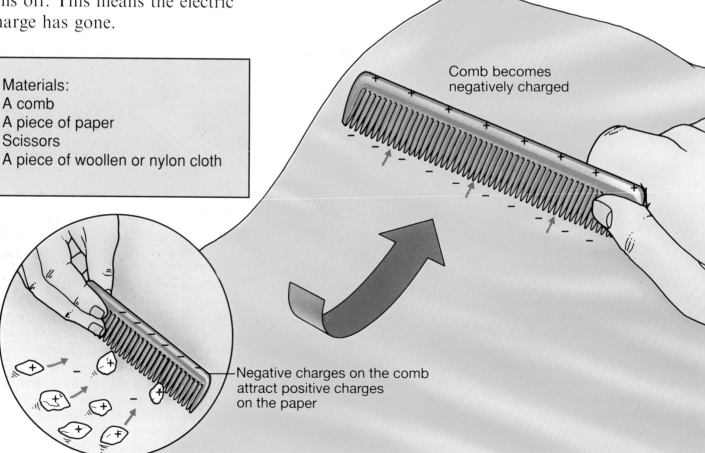

Comb becomes negatively charged

Negative charges on the comb attract positive charges on the paper

2. Measuring the wind

Meteorologists measure the speed of the wind using an instrument called an anemometer. The most common type of anemometer has three or four cups attached to spokes on a rotating shaft. As the wind blows, the spokes turn the shaft. The speed of the wind is indicated by the speed of the spinning shaft. Try making a simple type of anemometer that turns in the wind.

Materials:
A piece of card
A pair of compasses
A pencil
Scissors
Strong paper
3 jar tops
Sticky tape
A strip of red paper

Method:

1. Roll up strips of paper to make three tubes of equal length. Make one shorter, fatter paper tube, too.

2. Draw a circle on the card and cut it out. Attach the short paper tube to the base of the card with sticky tape.

3. Tape each of the longer tubes to one of the coffee jar lids. Now tape the tubes to the underside of the card circle, spacing them out evenly. Attach the strip of red paper to one lid.

4. Insert the pencil into the short paper tube, and make sure that the card circle spins easily.

5. Take your measuring instrument outside. Hold it up and allow it to turn freely in the wind. Count how many turns the red marker makes in one minute. Repeat this test in the same way at the same time each day for a week. Keep a record of your findings.

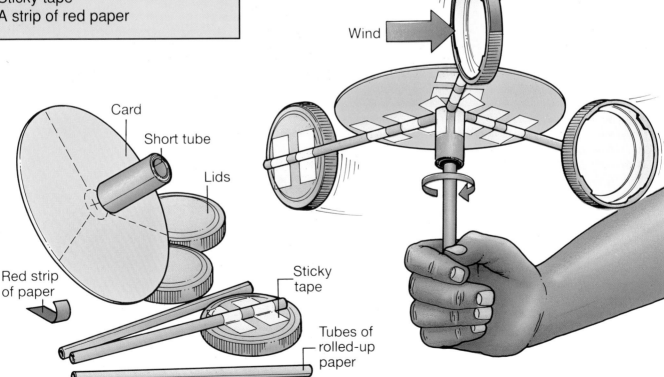

Card
Short tube
Lids
Red strip of paper
Sticky tape
Tubes of rolled-up paper
Wind

GLOSSARY

AIR CURRENT A movement of air.

AIR MASS A very large area of air with the same temperature throughout.

ATMOSPHERE The thin blanket of air that surrounds the Earth.

AVALANCHE A sudden fall of snow or ice down a slope.

CUMULONIMBUS A very large thundercloud that brings heavy rain, hail or snow.

DEATH TOLL The total number of people who die as the result of a disaster.

DELTA A triangular area of swampy land created where the mouth of a river branches into several streams.

DYSENTERY An infection of the intestine caused by drinking polluted water.

EVACUATION The movement of people out of an area because of war or disaster.

EYE The calm, central area of a hurricane.

FRONT The edge of an air mass.

HAILSTONE A small pellet of ice that falls from cumulonimbus clouds.

METEOROLOGIST A scientist who studies the weather.

NATURAL DISASTER Any terrible event resulting in deaths, injuries or damage to property which is not caused by human activity.

RADAR A system that locates distant objects by sending out radio waves and detecting them when they bounce back off the objects.

SLEET Falling snow or hail that has partly melted or partly frozen rain.

TROPOSPHERE The lower layer of the atmosphere where most weather occurs.

TYPHOID A dangerous infectious fever caused by drinking polluted water.

VEGETATION All the trees and plants that grow in a parficular area.

VISIBILITY The distance over which objects can be seen.

WALL CLOUDS Heavy clouds that form around the eye of a hurricane.

WEATHER SATELLITE A device that orbits the Earth and sends back scientific information about the weather.

THE POPULAR
POTATO
BEST RECIPES

VALWYN McMONIGAL

TORMONT

CONTENTS

4 All About Potatoes

6 Types, Preparation, and Cooking Techniques

14 Tasty Beginnings

56 Vegetarian Delights

64 Fabulous Fries

70 Fillings, Toppings and Stuffings

92 Glossary

94 Oven Temperatures, Measurements and Cup Measures

95 Index

88 Bubble and Squeak

90 How to Grow Your Own

24 Sensational Salads

34 Main Courses

46 Classic Accompaniments

76 Baking Day

82 Sweet Potatoes

86 Children's Special Spuds

Photography by Ashley Barber
Styling by Michelle Gorry

This edition is published with the permission of HarperCollins Publishers Pty Limited.

Published in 1994 by
Tormont Publications Inc.
338 Saint Antoine St. East
Montreal, Canada H2Y 1A3
Tel. (514) 954-1441
Fax (514) 954-1443
ISBN 2-89429-490-5
Printed in Canada

ACKNOWLEDGEMENTS
The publisher would like to thank the following for their help during the photography of this book:
Accoutrement; Appley Hoare Antiques; Corso de Fiori; Casa Shopping Exclusive Kitchen and Giftware; Chelsea House Antiques; Country Collection; Country Form Furniture; Dansab Pty Ltd; John Normyle; Laura Ashley (Aust) Pty Ltd; Lesolivades; Lifestyle Imports Pty Ltd; Made Where; Mikasa Tableware; Parterre Garden; Royal Doulton Australia Pty Ltd; Saywell Imports; Sydney Antique Centre; The Bay Tree; The Country Trader.

All About Potatoes

Historical Background

The potato has a remarkable history. It has been baked, boiled, steamed and mashed, used as a super-slimmers' food and loved by diabetics. It has also been blamed for causing leprosy and mass emigration, and its flowers have decorated royal coat lapels and crockery.

Colloquially known as the 'spud' — the name of the tool once used to weed the potato patch — the potato is one of the most popular staple foods in the world. Eaten since ancient times, it still graces most plates at least once a day in many countries.

The known history of potato cultivation in South America began 1800 years ago. Its introduction to Europe is more recent. In 1500 AD, the Spanish reached the Andes in Peru and christened the potato the 'batata', the West Indian name for the botanically quite distinct sweet potato.

Reports as to how potatoes reached Europe vary. Some claim they came in a Spanish Armada ship which foundered in Irish waters in the mid-16th century. Sir John Hawkins is reputed to have introduced the potato to England in 1563, but cultivation did not begin until Sir Francis Drake brought back another load of potatoes in 1586.

Popular history credits Sir Walter Raleigh with the introduction of potato cultivation in Ireland and the humble 'spud' reached the royal table in England in 1619. By the 18th century, the potato had travelled to North America, and was being grown in England, Scotland, Ireland, France and Germany.

The potato's reputation did suffer some blows on the way. In France, until the late 1700s, it was widely believed that the potato caused leprosy and fever. In 1773, the French scientist Parmentier wrote a thesis extolling the virtues of the potato. Following the success of a royal grant to encourage potato cultivation, King Louis XVI is reported to have worn a potato flower in his buttonhole.

Scorn turned to praise and the potato flower became highly fashionable, decorating everything from clothing to crockery. By the early 19th century, the potato had become a staple food in France.

The Irish also embraced the potato, so enthusiastically that their economy soon became dependent on it. The Irish potato crop of 1845–1847 failed disastrously due to blight, causing starvation and mass emigration to Australia and the United States. Settlers brought their love of potatoes with them and the development of new varieties and anti-fungal chemicals guaranteed continued cultivation.

The popularity of the potato has grown steadily over the years. Potatoes are used to make bread in many countries, eaten as a vegetable every day around the world, and, recently, restaurants specialising in every imaginable kind of potato dish have become spectacularly fashionable in London and New York.

Nutritional Value

One of the main reasons for the popularity of the potato is its excellent value. With a high water content, it makes a filling bulk food. It has a good ratio of proteins to calories and the quality of those proteins is high. There is also a high level of vitamins and minerals.

The average baked potato provides the recommended daily intake of riboflavin (B_2), three to four times the necessary amount of thiamin (B_1) and niacin (B_3), one and a half times the quantity of iron, and ten times the amount of vitamin C.

It has almost no fat or salt and offers more potassium than a banana. It is one of the easiest types of starch to assimilate and contains two and half times fewer carbohydrates than a similar quantity of bread, which makes the potato popular with diabetics.

It is also becoming a popular diet food. Because of traditional toppings such as sour cream and butter, the potato has developed a reputation as a no-no for weight watchers. In reality, a fair-sized baked potato (200 g) contains about the same number of kilojoules as an average apple or a glass of orange juice (about 300 kj).

POTATO TO FUEL THE CAR
Henry Ford in 1917 suggested that a potato from Europe which had a high-yielding alcohol content, should be grown and used in place of gasolene!

Types, Preparation, and Cooking Techniques

Types

The way potatoes are cooked is only limited by the cook's imagination. However, not all ways of cooking suit all types of potatoes; so the type of potato you buy should depend on how you plan to cook them.

Extensive research is being undertaken around the world and there are now literally hundreds of varieties: white, yellow, red, purple and lilac. What is available in your grocery store depends on where you live, however, as different varieties are grown in different countries.

Many people know the potatoes they buy only by the classifications of 'red', 'old' and 'new'. Red are usually a red-skinned type, such as Pontiac, but old and new refer to the stages of growth: new potatoes are the latest season's crop; old potatoes are held over from the previous year.

The following is a short list of some of the more popular varieties available:

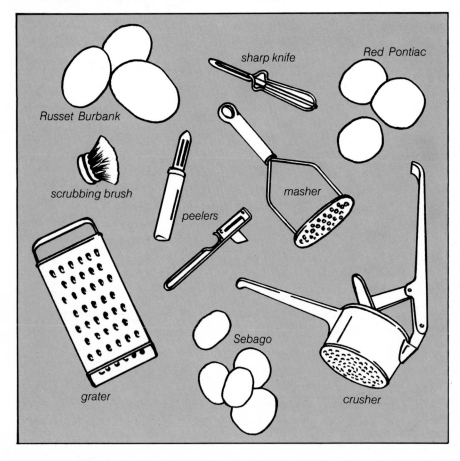

Russet Burbank · sharp knife · Red Pontiac · scrubbing brush · peelers · masher · grater · Sebago · crusher

6

WHAT POTATO IS THAT?					
TYPE	DESCRIPTION	PERFORMANCE IN			
		boiling	baking	frying	salads
American Burbank	long, oval, russet skin, white flesh	good	good	excel	fair
Craig Royal	red skin, creamy flesh	good	good	fair	good
Desiree	white skin, creamy flesh	good	good	good	good
Epicure	white skin, creamy flesh	excel	good	good	good
Home Guard	white skin, creamy flesh	excel	good	good	excel
King Edward	white skin, yellowish flesh	good	good	good	good
Majestic	creamy white flesh	good	good	good	good
Maris Peer	white skin, creamy white flesh	excel	good	good	good
Pentland Crown	white skin, oval	good	excel	good	good

American Burbank – a russet-coloured, waxy variety, excellent for chipping

Craig Royal — early variety with fine texture, very good boiled and in salads

Desiree — good all-purpose potato with pale creamy flesh and mealy texture

Epicure — early potato with distinctive flavour, excellent boiled, maintains its shape

Home Guard — one of the first early varieties, with a floury texture, very good boiled and for salads

King Edward — excellent general potato with mealy, creamy white flesh

Majestic — main-crop variety, good keeper, very good roasted, chipped, jacket baked

Maris Peer — early variety with firm texture, very good boiled, in salads and for chips

Pentland Crown — a waxy main crop variety suitable for boiling, sautés and salads

Nomenclature for varieties can be confusing, as it varies from country to country. In general, early varieties have a waxy texture, and are suitable for purees, chips and sautés. Storage time is limited. Main-crop potatoes may be either waxy (best for boiling and salads) or floury (preferable for roasting and chipping).

Buying and Storing

When buying potatoes it is important to choose firm, dry potatoes with unbroken skins, and which are free from sprouts and green patches. Uneven surfaces and eyes, however, cause no real harm. They simply make preparation time longer.

Green spots in potatoes result from exposure to light. The green colour indicates the presence of chlorophyll which could mean the existence of solanine, a toxin which has been known to cause illness. The green patches, which give the potato a bitter taste, can be cut out if they appear in small patches. Otherwise, the potato should be discarded.

The best way to store potatoes is unwashed (and dry) in a dark, cool, dry place. They should never be refrigerated (except for new potatoes). Store them away from onions, which speed up their spoilage. Once potatoes begin to sprout, show green patches, or go soft, they should be discarded.

New potatoes do not keep as well as the other varieties, and should be bought only in small quantities. They are at their best when their skin has a ragged appearance, and feels slightly moist.

Few people are aware that potatoes can be frozen for up to three months. Peel, wash and cut potatoes into chips; plunge into boiling water for two minutes, rinse thoroughly in cold water, dry and pack into plastic bags to freeze.

HANDY HINT
Retain water used to cook vegetables in refrigerator and use as stock in place of water. Vegetable water sealed or covered will keep in the refrigerator for 6 days, or frozen for 3 months.

Cooking Techniques

Careful preparation can make all the difference to the way your potatoes look and taste. Remove all green patches, bruises, eyes and any other marks. Peel potatoes evenly but not too deeply, as vitamins and minerals are stored in, and just below, the skin.

When dicing or slicing, make potato pieces the same size: this ensures even cooking and equal cooking time. To prepare perfect chips, see details on pages 66–67.

Boiling: This takes approximately 40 minutes (whole), 20 minutes (quartered), 12 minutes (diced). Cook potatoes in only a small quantity of boiling water, to avoid loss of nutrients. Cooking water can be kept to make a vitamin-rich soup or casserole. More vitamins and minerals are retained if you boil potatoes in their skins.

Baking: Potatoes can be placed directly on a rack in the oven or in a baking dish with a little oil or butter. This method takes approximately one hour on 200°C (400°F), and is another good way of retaining nutrients.

Oven Steaming: Pour a small amount of water into a pan, place potatoes on a rack over the water, and cover. This method takes about one hour on 200°C (400°F).

Pressure Cooking: This is an excellent way to retain colour and nutrients, and takes about one-third of the time it takes to boil potatoes.

Steaming: This method also preserves colour and nutrients but takes slightly longer than boiling. Place a small amount of boiling water in a pan, and arrange potatoes in a perforated container over the water. Time varies with size of potato, and whether you steam whole or quartered. If quartering, parboil briefly first, so potatoes don't break up.

POMMES
Spaniards often refer to the potato as "pommes" or "apples of love" due to the supposed aphrodisiac qualities.

Peel thinly, as vitamins are stored in and just below the skin.

Dice potatoes into the same sized pieces for even cooking.

9

Stewing and Casseroling: Potatoes should be placed with other vegetables or meat in a covered dish and either cooked on top of the hot plate, or in the oven on 180°C (350°F) for about one hour.

Frying: Shallow-frying is a great way to cook leftovers. The potatoes should be cooked in 2.5 cm of oil. Leftovers or thinly sliced potatoes can also be pan-fried in one tablespoon of oil or butter, and deep-frying gives us chips and French fries, increasingly popularised by chain stores throughout the world.

Microwaving: This is the most nutritious way to cook potatoes. If cooking them in their skin, prick them first to prevent them exploding from the build-up of steam and heated juices. When cooking more than one potato at a time, arrange them in a circle on a paper towel or in a microwave-safe dish, and rearrange from time to time to ensure even cooking. Choose similar-sized potatoes so they take the same amount of time to cook.

Slice potatoes the same thickness to ensure even cooking.

As every microwave oven is slightly different, and wattages can vary considerably, cooking times will also vary. Times given in our recipes are based on a 600 watt oven, so if your oven wattage is lower, increase cooking time slightly; if your wattage is higher, decrease cooking time slightly. Always undercook, test for taste and doneness, and if necessary, return to the oven briefly.

To boil potatoes in your microwave, scrub new potatoes and prick with a fork, but do not peel. Place in a wide-based dish with 1½ tablespoons of water. Old potatoes should be peeled, cut into quarters or slices, and placed in a dish with 3 tablespoons of water and a pinch of salt. Cover dishes with plastic cling wrap, rolled back at one edge. Stir once during cooking. Microwave on HIGH (100%) until tender. Leave new potatoes to stand 5 minutes and old potatoes for 3 minutes.

To stuff potatoes, scoop out cooked flesh and leave a 2.5 cm border.

POTATO COOKING TECHNIQUES

METHOD	TIME	TECHNIQUE
Boil	40 minutes (whole) 20 minutes (quartered) 12 minutes (diced)	Scrub well, peel if desired, and use only a small amount of boiling water for new potatoes, cold water for old. Add salt, if preferred, and cover.
Bake or roast	40–60 minutes	Peel, halve or quarter and arrange in a baking dish with a little oil or butter. Cook on 250°C (475°F).
Foil bake	40–60 minutes	Wash well, rub skins well with a little oil, wrap in foil and bake on 250°C (475°F).
Fry	18 minutes minimum	Slice potatoes finely, chill in a bowl of iced water 10 minutes minimum; drain. Heat deep-frying oil to 190°C (375°F), fry chips in a basket 5–8 minutes; drain. Raise oil temperature to 200°C (400°F), fry chips again, 3–5 minutes; drain well.
Jacket bake	40–60 minutes	Wash well, and place on a rack in the oven; bake at 200°C (400°F).
Mash	15 minutes	Wash, peel and dice; boil until just tender. Drain well and mash with butter, milk, salt and pepper, to taste.
Dry mash	15 minutes	Wash, peel and dice; boil until just tender and mash.
Microwave	1 minute per potato + 2 minutes standing time	To boil in skins: prick first, place in a dish, cover and microwave on HIGH (100%).
	6 minutes + 3–5 minutes standing time	To boil peeled and diced: place in a dish with 1 tablespoon water and a dash salt, cover with cling wrap leaving one corner turned back, stir once during cooking and microwave on HIGH (100%).
Steam	15 minutes	Place a small amount of water in a pan, arrange potatoes in a perforated container over water, cover and cook 5–7 minutes.
Oven steam	1 hour	Place small amount of water in a pan, arrange potatoes on a rack over water, cover and cook.

Perfect Potatoes

There are so many ways to make perfect potatoes, but all involve a few basic techniques. Once mastered, you can branch out and experiment with endless variations of your own.
On these two pages, you will find reliable recipes for *some classic potato dishes: baked, mashed, baked in foil and served with sour cream, potato cups and herbed potatoes with parsley and butter. These favourites can accompany almost any dish or make a snack on their own.*

HERBED POTATOES

2 small new potatoes per person, lightly scrubbed
1 teaspoon butter per 2 potatoes
½ tablespoon chopped fresh parsley or basil, per 2 potatoes

Place potatoes in a pan and just cover with boiling water. Bring to the boil and simmer until tender, approximately 20 minutes. (Alternatively prick potatoes with a fork, crowd into a small dish, cover with a lid or microwave wrap and microwave on HIGH, allowing 1 minute per potato. Stand 2 minutes.)

Drain. Melt butter in a pan, add parsley and potatoes, and coat potatoes well with parsley butter (or microwave butter with parsley on HIGH 1 minute. Remove from microwave, add potatoes and shake well to cover). Serve immediately.

TASTY VARIATION:
☐ Use ½ tablespoon per person of any chopped fresh herbs or a sprinkle of freshly ground black pepper, to taste.

BEST BAKED POTATOES

6 medium potatoes, peeled
2 tablespoons oil

Wash potatoes and stand in cold water for 30 minutes. Pat dry with kitchen paper towel. Cut potatoes lengthways in half.

Heat oil in a baking dish for 5 minutes. Add potatoes and bake at 250°C (475°F) for 20 minutes. Turn potatoes over. Bake a further 20 minutes or until golden. Drain on kitchen paper towel to absorb excess oil. Serve immediately.

Serves 6

IDAHO JACKET POTATOES

oil
6 large new potatoes, washed and dried

TO SERVE
½ cup sour cream, natural yoghurt or cottage cheese (125 mL)
2 tablespoons freshly chopped chives or fresh parsley, or
1 rasher bacon, finely diced or shredded

Rub a little oil over each potato and wrap in a square of aluminium foil.

Arrange on a baking tray and bake at 250°C (475°F) for 40 minutes or until tender (or wrap potatoes in microwave wrap and microwave on HIGH 10–12 minutes; stand 2 minutes).

Remove foil or wrap and cut a criss-cross pattern across the top of each potato. Gently squeeze potato until the top opens out. Serve with a dollop of sour cream, natural yoghurt or cottage cheese and top with chives, bacon or parsley.

Serves 6

POTATO CUPS

These are great served with a salad, as a light snack or as an accompaniment for barbeques, buffets, and even a special dinner party. Allow 1–2 potatoes per person.

**medium old potatoes
oil**

Scrub the skins to remove dirt and prick with a skewer several times. Place potatoes apart on a rack and bake at 180°C (350°F) for 1 hour or until tender (or microwave on HIGH 10 minutes).

Cool sufficiently so you can handle them. Cut in half and scoop out the pulp leaving a 1-cm thick shell. Dry mash the potato pulp and set aside to use in filling of your choice (see Fillings recipes).

Brush potatoes inside and out with oil and arrange on a greased oven tray, cut side up. Bake at 200°C (400°F) for 10 minutes (microwaving will not crisp the shells, so ignore this step).

Potatoes are now ready for filling.

HEALTHY FILLING

**6 Potato Cups (see recipe)
4 tablespoons natural (unflavoured) yoghurt or cottage cheese
1 tablespoon chopped fresh parsley or mint**

Prepare potato cups, reserving mashed potato pulp. Combine all ingredients. Spoon into shells and reheat.

Fills 6 potatoes

SIZE OF POTATOES
Most of the recipes in our book specify what size potato to use. Those that don't leave it to your discretion. In general, the following sizes may be useful:

large 200 grams
medium 150 grams
small 100 grams

MASHED
If mashing, allow 1½ medium-sized potatoes per person, or 2–3 new potatoes, depending on size.

BAKING POTATOES WITH ROASTS
When cooking baked potatoes with a joint of meat, don't place potatoes under the meat as the juices will soften the potatoes and they will not crisp. Either arrange around the meat or cook in a separate dish in the top part of the oven.

Potatoes make ideal accompaniments. Try Herbed Potatoes, Best Roast Potatoes, Baked Idaho Potatoes and Potato Cups with Healthy Filling.

Tasty Beginnings

Soups and starters make fabulous first courses, light meals or tempting snacks. In the following selection, you can also find ideal party food, easy to hand around on trays or arrange as a smorgasbord.

TARAMOSALATA

4 thick slices white bread
warm water
1 medium potato, peeled, cooked and dry mashed
125 g tarama (see Glossary)
1 clove garlic, crushed
½ small onion, peeled and grated
1 egg, separated
¼ cup lemon juice (60 mL)
¼–½ cup olive oil (60–125 mL)
black olives and crusty breadstick, to serve

Cut crusts from bread slices, put bread in a bowl and cover with warm water for 3 minutes. Drain and gently squeeze bread by hand to remove water.

In a blender or processor, combine potato, tarama, garlic and onion. Blend until smooth. Gradually add egg yolk, lemon juice and sufficient oil for a thick, smooth consistency. If beating by hand, also add egg white to the mixture and beat very well with a spoon.

Spoon mixture into a serving bowl and chill thoroughly. Serve accompanied by olives and breadstick.

Serves 6

TASTY VARIATION:
☐ Taramosalata also goes well with Cucumber Dip (see recipe) served in separate bowls; or with raw vegetables, such as cucumber and celery sticks, radishes, sliced mushrooms and cauliflower florets.

CUCUMBER DIP

200 g natural (unflavoured) yoghurt
1 cucumber, peeled and grated
1 clove garlic, crushed
1 shallot, finely diced

Combine all ingredients and chill thoroughly in a serving bowl.

Serves 4–6

DEEP-FRIED VEGETABLES WITH TOMATO DIP

BATTER
1 cup chick pea or self-raising flour (125 g)
½ teaspoon chilli powder
½ teaspoon bicarbonate of soda
water, to mix

TOMATO DIP
1 cup tomato puree (250 mL)
300 mL natural (unflavoured) yoghurt
¼ teaspoon ground cumin
1 tablespoon chopped fresh parsley

VEGETABLES
1 potato, peeled and sliced
1 eggplant, peeled and thinly sliced
1 onion, sliced
1 green capsicum, seeded and sliced
4 cauliflower florets
oil, for deep-frying

To make the batter, combine flour, chilli powder and bicarbonate of soda together. Whisk in sufficient water to make a smooth batter.

To make the tomato dip, combine all the dip ingredients in a serving bowl.

Dip all the vegetables into batter. Fry in hot oil until golden brown and drain on kitchen paper towel. To serve, arrange fried vegetables on a platter with the tomato dip.

Serves 6

Deep-fried Vegetables with Tomato Dip, Taramosalata and Cucumber Dip

POTATO STICKS

1 large potato, peeled and cooked
2 egg yolks
40 g butter
1 cup self-raising flour (125 g)
pepper, to taste
1 tablespoon chopped fresh chives
1 egg, beaten
sesame seeds, to garnish

Mash potato with egg yolks and butter until creamy. Beat in flour, pepper and chives to form a dough. Chill for 1 hour.

On a floured board roll out dough to a 1 cm thickness. Cut 6 cm long, 1 cm wide strips. Twist, brush lightly with beaten egg and sprinkle with sesame seeds. Bake for 10 minutes at 200°C (400°F) until crisp and brown. Cool and serve as hors d'oeuvres.

TASTY VARIATION:
☐ Instead of sesame seeds, use grated cheese or caraway seeds, to taste.

Serves 2

Fettuccine with Potato and Tomato Sauce

FETTUCCINE WITH POTATO AND TOMATO SAUCE

500 g fettuccine, cooked

SAUCE
20 g butter
2 shallots, diced
2 celery stalks, diced
½ green capsicum, diced
1 zucchini, diced
1 large potato, peeled and diced
4 rashers bacon, diced
425 g canned tomatoes, liquid reserved
1 cup water (250 mL)
1 chicken stock cube
pinch dried thyme
1 clove garlic, crushed

Melt butter, add all vegetables and bacon and gently fry until bacon fat runs clear. Add all remaining ingredients including tomato liquid. Bring to the boil and simmer for 30 minutes. (Alternatively, microwave butter, shallots and bacon on HIGH 2 minutes. Add diced potato and cook 2 minutes. Add remaining ingredients and microwave on HIGH 10 minutes). Serve with cooked fettuccine.

Serves 6

BAKED OR FRIED POTATO SKINS WITH AIOLI SAUCE DIP

Yes! even the humble potato skin can be used — and with scrumptious results.

6 medium potatoes
40 g melted butter (for baked skins)
coarse salt
oil, for deep-frying (for fried skins)

AIOLI SAUCE DIP
cooked pulp of 2 medium potatoes
8 cloves garlic, crushed
1 cup virgin olive oil (250 mL)
1 egg yolk
1 teaspoon lemon juice

Scrub potatoes, rinse well and pat dry. Pierce the skins several times with a fork. Bake in a 180°C (350°F) oven for 45–60 minutes or until tender (or microwave on HIGH 8 minutes, stand 4 minutes). Cool slightly, cut in half and scoop out flesh, leaving a 1 cm thick shell. Put aside pulp from 2 of the potatoes to use in the Aioli Sauce Dip. Using a sharp knife, cut each shell lengthways into eight equal sections.

For baked skins, brush inside and out with melted butter and sprinkle with coarse salt. Place on a baking sheet and bake in a 250°C (475°F) oven for 10–12 minutes until crisp.

For fried skins, heat oil and fry skins until crisp. Drain on kitchen paper towels.

To prepare the sauce, combine potato pulp, garlic and half the oil in a blender. Blend till smooth. Add egg yolk and slowly add remaining oil and the lemon juice. To make the sauce without a blender, mash potato, add garlic and beat in one-quarter of the oil, all the egg yolk and lemon juice. Slowly beat in remaining oil. This method will take about 10 minutes. If sauce is too thick, add 2 teaspoons hot water. Serve sauce in a dip bowl surrounded by potato skins.

Serves 6

TASTY VARIATIONS:
Replace Aioli Sauce Dip with:
☐ 250 mL sour cream mixed with 2 tablespoons chopped fresh chives; or
☐ 250 g cottage cheese with 60 g diced smoked salmon.

CRUSHING GINGER
For a time-saving trick, use a garlic crusher to crush fresh ginger.

AVOCADO FARCI

6 medium potatoes, washed and dried
40 g butter
2 ripe avocados, peeled and sliced
1 tablespoon lemon juice

FILLING
40 g butter
1 tablespoon flour
1 teaspoon powdered chicken stock
1 teaspoon curry powder
1 cup milk (250 mL)
225 g canned salmon or tuna, drained and bones removed

Bake potatoes in a 180°C (350°F) oven for 1 hour (or microwave on HIGH 8 minutes, stand for 4 minutes). Remove from oven or microwave, and cool. Cut one-third from the top of each potato and scoop out potato pulp, leaving 1 cm thick shell.

Melt 40 g butter in a saucepan (or microwave on HIGH 30 seconds) and brush over the outside of potato shells. Crisp shells in a 180°C (350°F) oven for 15 minutes. This step must be done in a conventional oven.

While shells are crisping, prepare filling. Melt 40 g butter in a saucepan and stir in flour, chicken stock and curry powder. Stir for 1 minute over medium heat, making sure there are no lumps. Remove from heat and stir in milk. Return to heat, stirring until mixture boils and thickens. Add salmon.

(Alternatively, microwave butter on HIGH 30 seconds. Stir in flour, chicken stock, curry powder and microwave on HIGH 1 minute. Beat in milk. Microwave on HIGH 2 minutes or until mixture boils and thickens. Stir well, then add salmon).

Fill the potato shells with salmon mixture and top with avocado slices sprinkled with lemon juice to prevent browning. Return to 180°C (350°F) oven for 15 minutes to heat through (or microwave on HIGH 2–4 minutes).

Serves 6

TASTY VARIATION:
☐ Sprinkle grated cheese over the top and brown under griller or in oven before serving.

Avocado Farci

LEMON JUICE
Always sprinkle fruits, such as avocado, bananas and apple, with lemon juice to prevent browning. Prepare as close to serving time as possible and the fruit will look luscious when it reaches the table.

Chilled soups are delightful served for an al fresco summer lunch or dinner.

CURRIED POTATO SOUP

This soup tastes especially good served with parsley sprigs set in ice cubes.

40 g butter
3 onions, sliced
6 medium potatoes, peeled and sliced
1 tablespoon curry powder
2 chicken stock cubes
1 tablespoon tamarind sauce (see
** *Note*)**
2 cups water (500 mL)
6 ice cubes with parsley sprig set in
** them (optional)**

Melt butter, add onions and gently fry till transparent. Add potatoes, curry powder, crumbled stock cubes, tamarind sauce and cover with water. Bring to the boil and simmer for 30 minutes. Blend or push through a sieve. Chill thoroughly before serving.

Serves 4

Note: Tarmarind sauce can be replaced by 1 tablespoon lemon juice.

GREEN HERB SOUP

20 g butter
6 shallots, whites and greens sliced
1 large potato, peeled and diced
4 outer lettuce leaves, washed and
** torn into small pieces**
2 cups water (500 mL)
juice ½ lemon
pepper, to taste
2 tablespoons chopped fresh herbs
** (see *Note*)**
½ cup cream (125 mL)

Melt butter, add shallots and gently fry until tender (or microwave butter and shallots together on HIGH 1 minute). Add diced potato and stir for 1 minute (or microwave on HIGH 30 seconds, then place in a pan). Add lettuce to the pan. Cover with water and bring to the boil. Simmer for 20 minutes. Stir in lemon juice and pepper, then if using a blender, add herbs and blend until smooth or if pushing soup through a sieve, add herbs after. Add cream and chill.

Serves 6

Note: Use any fresh herbs, or a mixture of herbs: basil, parsley, mint, thyme, rosemary, sage, sorrel, etc.

Curried Potato Soup and Green Herb Soup

CUCUMBER AND LIME SOUP

1 large cucumber, peeled, seeded and sliced
3 medium potatoes, peeled and sliced
2 shallots, diced
1 cup water (250 mL)
juice 3 limes
½ cup cream (125 mL)
cucumber or lime twists, to garnish

Combine cucumber, potatoes, shallots, water and lime juice in a pan. Bring to the boil and simmer for 30 minutes. Blend till smooth or push through a sieve. Stir in cream and chill thoroughly. Serve in six wide champagne glasses with a twist of cucumber or lime.

Serves 6

SATAY SAUCE

20 g butter
1 medium onion, peeled and diced
½ teaspoon chilli powder
pepper, to taste
3 tablespoons sugar
4 tablespoons peanut butter
¼ cup white vinegar (60 mL)
2 teaspoons soy sauce
1 cup water (250 mL)

Heat butter in a pan, add onion and gently fry till tender. Add remaining ingredients, simmer for 10–12 minutes or until thick, then serve.

(Alternatively combine butter and onion and microwave on HIGH 2 minutes. Add remaining ingredients and microwave on HIGH 2 minutes or until mixture thickens.)

This sauce will keep refrigerated in a covered jar for up to two weeks.

Makes approximately 1¼ cups (310 mL)

SPICY POTATO PUFFS

4 tablespoons vegetable oil
1 clove garlic, crushed
1 medium onion, peeled and sliced
1 tablespoon chopped fresh coriander leaves
1 tablespoon ground turmeric
pepper, to taste
1 tablespoon sugar
500 g minced chicken or pork
1 large potato, cooked and dry mashed
1 shallot, finely diced
1 kg prepared puff pastry
oil, for deep-frying
satay sauce, bought or homemade (see recipe), to serve

Spicy Potato Puffs are easy to make: mix up filling ingredients, roll dough into circles, spoon on filling, and fold dough, pinching edges together to form a decorative edge.

Heat oil in a wok or frying pan. Fry garlic until golden brown. Add onion, coriander and turmeric and stir for 1 minute. Add pepper, sugar and minced chicken. Stir until meat has browned. Stir in mashed potato and shallot, then remove from heat. Allow to cool.

Cut each pastry sheet into four 10 cm squares. In the centre of each square, place a spoonful of the mixture. Fold pastry into a triangle, pinching edges together with your fingers to form a curly edge. Place each triangle on a sheet of greaseproof paper dusted with flour. Repeat until all the pastry and filling

> **POTATO PULP**
> Potato pulp can be covered or put in an airtight container and stored in the refrigerator for three days.

are used. Refrigerate until ready to use.

Heat deep-frying oil. When hot, fry each triangle until golden brown then drain. Set aside in a warm oven while frying the remaining puffs, a few at a time. Serve with Satay Sauce (see recipe).

Makes approximately 24 triangles

Handy hint: Make the puffs in advance and freeze them uncooked. To use, thaw then fry.

TASTY VARIATION:
☐ Use 500 g of any leftover meats, minced chicken, lamb or beef.

> **ICE CUBES**
> For a professional touch, serve chilled summer soups with ice cubes set with a sprig of fresh parsley or another favourite herb, fresh from your garden.

SEAFOOD IN A BASKET

500 g uncooked (green) prawns, shelled and deveined
500 g fish fillets, cut in 2.5 cm pieces
2 tablespoons lemon juice
250 g scallops
2 tablespoons milk
2 tablespoons oil
½ teaspoon sesame seed oil
250 g snow peas, topped and tailed
2 tablespoons Hoisin sauce

POTATO BASKETS
6 large potatoes, peeled and coarsely grated
2 tablespoons cornflour
oil, for deep-frying

Cut prawns lengthways in half. Combine prawns and fish in a bowl and pour over lemon juice. Put scallops in another bowl and cover with milk. Allow both to marinate while you make the baskets.

Pat potatoes dry with kitchen paper towels. In a bowl combine grated potatoes with cornflour. Lightly oil a medium and small strainer. Place one-sixth of the potato mixture in the medium strainer. Press the small strainer onto the potato to form the shape of a cup. Heat oil until very hot. Holding both the strainer handles tightly, lower the strainers into the hot oil. Cook until the potato is golden and tap out onto an oven tray. Repeat until you have six baskets. Keep the baskets hot in a 180°C (350°F) oven while cooking the seafood.

Heat both the oils in a wok or frying pan, add the drained seafood and stir-fry for 2 minutes. Add snow peas and Hoisin sauce. Stir-fry a further 30 seconds. To serve, position a potato basket on each plate and fill with seafood mix.

Serves 6

Note: Similar in appearance to barbecue sauce, Hoisin sauce is a thick red, spicy sauce made from soy beans, garlic and onion. Available from supermarkets and delicatessens, it is used to flavour vegetables, shellfish and duck.

TASTY VARIATIONS:
☐ Replace Hoisin sauce with 1–2 tablespoons of soy sauce;
☐ for an extra nutty flavour, fry 20 g almond halves with the snow peas.

1. Combine potatoes and cornflour.

2. Place one-sixth of mixture in medium strainer.

20

3. Press small strainer into potato to form a cup shape.

4. Holding handles tightly, lower strainers into hot oil.

5. To serve, fill each potato basket with seafood mixture.

Crab Mornay

CREAMY SCALLOP SOUP

250 g scallops
1 cup milk (250 mL)
500 g fish fillets
1 litre water
1 cup white wine (250 mL)
40 g butter
1 onion, sliced
2 medium potatoes, peeled and sliced
2 egg yolks beaten with
  3 tablespoons cream
crusty bread, to serve

Trim the orange roe from the scallops and set aside. Dice the white part and cover with milk in a bowl. Arrange fish in a frying pan with water and wine. Bring to the boil, lower heat and simmer for 30 minutes. Remove fish, flake, discard bones and set fish aside. Reserve cooking liquid.

Melt butter in a pan and lightly fry onion; add sliced potatoes and fish cooking liquid. Bring to the boil, lower heat and simmer 30 minutes.

In another pan, simmer scallops and milk without boiling for 4 minutes only.

Blend or push through a sieve, flaked fish, scallops and milk, onions, potatoes and fish cooking liquid. Stir in combined egg yolks and cream.

To serve, reheat without boiling, stirring all the time (or microwave on HIGH until soup starts to steam). Serve in a tureen or in soup bowls, with crusty bread.

Serves 8

CRAB MORNAY

40 g butter
4 shallots, chopped
1 tablespoon flour
½ cup milk (125 mL)
¼ cup white wine (60 mL)
2 teaspoons French mustard
400 g canned red crabmeat, drained
½ cup cream (125 mL)

TOPPING
4 medium potatoes, peeled and
  cooked
dash milk and butter, for mashing
grated cheese, to taste
6 slices lemon and chopped fresh
  parsley, to serve

Melt butter in a pan and fry shallots until tender. Add flour and cook for 1 minute, stirring continually. Remove from heat, stir in milk, wine and French mustard. Return to heat and bring to the boil stirring all the time. Add crabmeat and cream.

(Alternatively, combine butter and shallots and microwave on HIGH 2 minutes. Stir in flour and microwave on HIGH 1 minute. Stir in milk, wine and mustard, and microwave on HIGH 2 minutes. Stir well and add crabmeat and cream.)

Spoon mixture into six entree dishes or a large baking dish.

To make the topping, mash cooked potatoes with milk and butter. Spread over crab mixture and sprinkle with grated cheese. Brown under griller (or microwave on HIGH until cheese melts). Garnish with lemon slices and parsley.

Serves 6

TASTY VARIATION:
☐ Replace crabmeat with 400 g of any seafood, freshly cooked or canned.

SEAFOOD
Never boil seafood — it becomes tough. Follow recipe instructions carefully: they may specify boiling prawn shells or heads for example; seafood flesh such as prawn meat or scallops, should be simmered gently on low heat, to cook slowly.

VICHYSSOISE

2 leeks
iced water
40 g butter
2 large potatoes, peeled and sliced
2 chicken stock cubes
2 cups water (500 mL)
300 mL cream

Slice the white part of the leeks and finely shred the green tops. Cover the green tops with iced water to curl.

Melt butter, add white part of leeks and fry until soft (or microwave on HIGH 2 minutes). Add potatoes, stock cubes and water, and bring to the boil. Lower heat and simmer for 30 minutes. Blend soup until smooth or push through a sieve. Stir in cream and chill thoroughly. Serve in six glass bowls garnished with the curly leek tops.

Serves 6

SCAMPI OR PRAWNS IN GARLIC SAUCE

4 medium potatoes, peeled and cooked
2 egg yolks
¼ cup milk (60 mL)
20 g butter

GARLIC SAUCE
12 uncooked scampi or 24 prawns (see Note)
1 cup white wine (250 mL)
40 g butter
1 small onion, peeled and sliced
2 cloves garlic, crushed
1 tablespoon flour
½ cup milk (125 mL)
½ cup cream (125 mL)
1 tablespoon chopped fresh parsley

Mash potatoes with egg yolks, milk and 20 g butter to a creamy texture.

Lightly grease six ovenproof entree plates with a little extra butter. Put a spoonful of potato mixture on each plate and, using a fork, make a 'nest'. Place plates in an oven preheated to 180°C (350°F). (Alternatively, spoon potato mixture on to plates and microwave on HIGH 2 minutes.)

To prepare sauce, break off the scampi heads, remove the shells and devein. Combine scampi heads and wine in a saucepan and bring to the boil. Boil until liquid is reduced by one-third. Strain, reserving liquid.

Melt 40 g butter in a saucepan, add onion and gently fry until tender, but not brown. Add garlic, stir in flour and cook for 1 minute, making sure there are no lumps. Remove from heat. Stir in milk and reserved wine. Return to heat and, constantly stirring, bring mixture to boil and allow to thicken. Add scampi, carefully stirring until scampi turn a pale pink. Do not allow mixture to boil. Gently stir in cream and parsley. Reheat without boiling.

(Alternatively, combine 40 g butter, the onion and garlic and microwave on HIGH 1 minute. Add flour and cook on HIGH 1 minute. Gradually add wine and milk, stirring until smooth and microwave on HIGH 2 minutes or until mixture boils and thickens. Stir well. Add scampi, cream and parsley and microwave on MEDIUM 1 minute.)

To serve, remove plates from oven or microwave and, with a slotted spoon, place two scampi into each 'nest'. Carefully spoon sauce over scampi.

Serves 6

Note: Scampi are very large prawns, originally from the Adriatic Sea and much used in Italian cooking. If unavailable, substitute any large, uncooked prawns .

Prawns in Beer Batter

PRAWNS IN BEER BATTER

2 large potatoes, cooked and creamed
18 uncooked (green) prawns
1 cup flour (125 g)
½ can beer (185 mL)
oil, for deep-frying

SAUCE
3 slices fresh or canned pineapple, finely chopped
1 cup mayonnaise (250 mL)
2 teaspoons curry powder

Spoon creamed potatoes into an ovenproof bowl. Warm in an oven preheated to 180°C (350°F), (or microwave on HIGH 2 minutes just before serving).

Shell prawns, leaving their tails on, and devein. Combine flour and beer in a bowl and mix to a smooth batter. If the mixture is too thick, stir in a little water.

Heat the oil. Holding a prawn by the tail, dip it into the batter then carefully fry until golden brown. Remove and drain on kitchen paper towels. Repeat until all prawns are cooked.

To make the sauce, combine pineapple, mayonnaise and curry powder in a bowl. Divide between six small bowls, arranged in the centre of six entree plates.

To serve, pipe or spoon the hot creamed potato around the sauce bowls. Position three prawns on each potato bed with the tails pointing outwards.

Alternatively, spoon creamed potato into bowls, arrange prawns decoratively on top, and serve sauce separately.

Serves 6

TASTY VARIATION:
☐ For a tropical touch, after the prawns have been dipped in batter, roll in shredded coconut and then fry.

Sensational Salads

Delicious meals that are good for you as well — these recipes are perfect for festive summer lunches or light family meals with a difference. Combine potatoes with a variety of ingredients, such as chicken, seafood, crispy vegetables and fresh fruit, pour over a favourite dressing and you have an easy-to-prepare dish for the whole family.

DILL-MUSTARD POTATO SALAD

**2 litres chicken stock
1 kg new baby potatoes, unpeeled
¾ cup vegetable oil (180 mL)
1 egg, room temperature
3 tablespoons Dijon-style mustard
2 tablespoons finely chopped fresh
   dill or 2 teaspoons dried
1 teaspoon red wine vinegar
1 teaspoon lemon juice
freshly ground black pepper
½ cup sour cream (125 mL)
3 celery stalks, thinly sliced
1 onion, thinly sliced
½ bunch chives, snipped**

Combine stock and potatoes and bring to boil over high heat. Reduce heat and cook potatoes just until tender. Drain immediately and rinse with cold water to cool. Drain potatoes well.

In a food processor or blender combine 3 tablespoons oil with the egg, mustard, dill, vinegar, lemon juice and pepper and blend until mixture is slightly thickened, about 10 seconds. With machine running, slowly pour in remaining oil in a thin, steady stream. Mix well. Add sour cream and blend 3 seconds to combine.

Slice potatoes into quarters and arrange in a salad bowl with celery and onion. Pour over the dressing and fold through the salad. Cover and refrigerate until ready to serve. Garnish with chives.

Serves 6

POTATO SALAD WITH PESTO MAYONNAISE

**1.5 kg small new potatoes
salt
3 tablespoons pine nuts
fresh basil leaves**

PESTO MAYONNAISE
**3 egg yolks
1 teaspoon Dijon-style mustard
1 tablespoon white wine vinegar
3 cloves garlic, peeled
1½ cups olive oil (375 mL)
salt and pepper, to taste
½ bunch fresh basil leaves
3 tablespoons parsley leaves
¼ cup grated Parmesan cheese (30g)**

Wash and scrub potatoes if necessary. Cook in boiling, salted water until just tender, about 20 minutes depending on their size. Drain and cool.

To make Pesto Mayonnaise, place egg yolks in a container with mustard, vinegar and garlic. Blend until smooth. Still blending, add the oil in a slow steady stream, until a thick mayonnaise has formed. Season well with salt and pepper. Add basil and parsley leaves, blend again until smooth. Add Parmesan cheese and blend until combined.

Fold mayonnaise through just warm potatoes and spoon into a serving bowl. Lightly toast pine nuts in a dry frying pan and sprinkle over the potato salad. Decorate with fresh basil leaves.

Serves 4–6

Sliced Potatoes Vinaigrette, Potato Salad with Pesto Mayonnaise, and Dill Mustard Potato Salad

BASIC POTATO SALAD

2 litres chicken stock
1 kg pontiac potatoes, peeled
3 tablespoons fresh mint sprigs

DRESSING
1 cup mayonnaise (250 mL)
½ cup sour cream (125 mL)
freshly ground black pepper
½ teaspoon mustard powder

Bring stock to the boil in a large saucepan. Add potatoes and mint and cook for 15 minutes or until just tender. Drain and cool potatoes then cut into 1.5 cm cubes.

Combine dressing ingredients. Place potatoes in a salad bowl and fold through dressing. Cover and refrigerate before serving.

Serves 4–6

POTATO SALAD WITH SPICY MAYONNAISE

Basic Potato Salad (see recipe)

SPICY MAYONNAISE
1 cup mayonnaise
½ cup sour cream (125 mL)
freshly ground black pepper
½ teaspoon mustard powder

Combine all the mayonnaise ingredients. Place potatoes in a salad bowl and fold through the dressing. Cover and refrigerate before serving.

Serves 4–6

SLICED POTATOES VINAIGRETTE

1 kg red new potatoes, unpeeled

VINAIGRETTE
6 tablespoons chopped fresh parsley
4 tablespoons freshly snipped chives
¾ cup safflower oil (180 mL)
¼ cup red wine vinegar (60 mL)
2 teaspoons dry mustard
1 teaspoon salt
freshly ground pepper

Cook potatoes until they can be pierced through with a sharp knife (do not overcook). Drain and cover with cold water. Let stand 12 minutes and drain again.

Combine finely chopped parsley and chives in a bowl. Add oil, vinegar and seasonings and whisk to blend.

Slice potatoes into vinaigrette. Invert mixture into serving bowl. Toss gently to coat potatoes evenly, adjust seasoning and serve at room temperature.

Serves 8

Basic Potato Salad
1. Cool potatoes with stock and mint.

2. Drain and cool potatoes in a colander.

3. Cut potatoes into cubes.

4. Combine dressing ingredients in a bowl.

5. Place potatoes in a salad bowl and fold through dressing.

CHICKEN SALAD

500 g chicken, diced and cooked
½ fresh pineapple, peeled and diced
2 shallots, diced
1 mandarin, segmented
Basic Potato Salad (see recipe)
3 tablespoons French Dressing
** (see recipe)**
lettuce leaves, washed
2 hardboiled eggs, shelled
** and chopped**
2 tomatoes, sliced
1 stalk celery, diced
3 tablespoons Tasty Mayonnaise
** (see recipe)**
20 g butter
2 tablespoons almond slivers

In a bowl combine chicken, pineapple, shallots, mandarin segments and potato salad. Stir through French Dressing.

Place lettuce leaves on a large plate. Spoon on chicken salad. Combine eggs, tomatoes, celery and mayonnaise and spoon mixture on top of chicken. Melt butter and fry almonds until lightly browned. Sprinkle almonds on top of salad and chill thoroughly.

Serves 6

TASTY VARIATION:
☐ Replace chicken with 500 g cooked prawns, shelled.

CURRIED POTATO SALAD

3 hardboiled eggs, shelled and sliced
2 stalks celery, diced
1 small capsicum, seeded and diced
Basic Potato Salad (see recipe)
1 tablespoon curry powder
Tasty Mayonnaise (see recipe)

In a bowl combine eggs, celery, capsicum and potato salad. Mix curry powder with mayonnaise, pour over salad and serve.

Serves 6

FESTIVE POTATO SALAD

8 medium mushrooms, washed
** and diced**
5 tablespoons French Dressing
** (see recipe)**
6 potatoes, peeled, diced and cooked
2 green apples, cored and sliced
juice 1 lemon
1 orange, peeled and segmented
2 hardboiled eggs, shelled and sliced
1 carrot, scraped and grated
6 small pickled onions
1 stalk celery, diced
2 tomatoes, sliced
lettuce cups

Place diced mushrooms in a salad bowl with French dressing and stand for at least 2 hours, preferably overnight. Add potatoes to mushrooms and dressing.

Add sliced apples and squeeze lemon juice over to prevent browning. Add all other ingredients. Chill and serve in lettuce cups.

Serves 6

JANSSONS TEMPTATION

This is a traditional Swedish recipe. As Sweden is home of the smorgasborg – the buffet style of serving where food is not heaped on the plate, but sampled one or two dishes at a time – this is a very appropriate dish for the casual or formal barbecue.

6 medium potatoes, peeled
2 onions, sliced
10 anchovies, cleaned or
** 20 canned anchovies**
450 mL cream
40 g butter

Slice potatoes into strips 1.5 cm thick. Grease a casserole dish and place one-third of potato strips on base. Top with half the onion and half the anchovies. Repeat, finishing with potatoes.

Pour 300 mL cream over and dot with butter. Bake at 180°C (350°F) for 45 minutes. Before serving, pour over 150 mL remaining cream. Serve with all barbecue meats and fish.

Serves 6

TASTY VARIATION:
☐ Replace anchovies with 210 g canned tuna, drained.

ITALIAN POTATO SALAD

2 cloves garlic, crushed
½ green capsicum, seeded and diced
½ red capsicum, seeded and diced
12 black olives
12 green olives
4 slices prosciutto ham cut into strips
125 g tasty cheese, diced
Basic Potato Salad (see recipe)
Vinaigrette (see recipe)

Combine all salad ingredients in a bowl and chill. Pour over vinaigrette and serve.

Serves 6

SALAD NIÇOISE

1 lettuce, washed
Vinaigrette (see recipe)
4 potatoes, peeled, sliced and cooked
125 g green beans, sliced and cooked
1 onion, finely diced
1 small cucumber, diced
6 tomatoes, quartered
12 black olives
2 hardboiled eggs, quartered
200 g canned tuna, drained
1 teaspoon freshly squeezed
** lemon juice**
12 anchovy fillets
1 tablespoon chopped fresh parsely

Arrange lettuce leaves in a salad bowl. Sprinkle with a little Vinaigrette. Arrange a layer of cold potatoes with beans and onion on top. Sprinkle with dressing. Add another layer cucumber, tomatoes, olives and eggs. Sprinkle with dressing. Add lemon juice to tuna, break into flakes and add to salad. Decorate top with a lattice effect of anchovy fillets and parsley. Serve chilled (do not allow to stand too long).

Serves 6

CANNED OR FRESH
220 g canned pineapple pieces or 220 g canned mandarin segments may be substituted for fresh.

Salad Niçoise

TASTY MAYONNAISE

3 egg yolks
½ cup virgin olive oil (125 mL)
3 tablespoons freshly squeezed
** lemon juice**
1 teaspoon sugar
3 tablespoons cream
1 tablespoon French mustard

Beat egg yolks in blender. Gradually beat in oil, lemon juice and sugar and blend on high speed until mixture is smooth. Add cream and mustard, blend 30 seconds, then chill.

If a blender is not used, beat egg yolks, add oil drop by drop beating well, then add lemon juice, beat again, add sugar, cream and mustard and beat until smooth.

Makes approximately 1¼ cups (310 mL)

FRENCH DRESSING

3 tablespoons white vinegar
pepper, to taste
½ teaspoon sugar
½ teaspoon dry mustard
1 clove garlic, crushed
½ cup virgin olive oil (125 mL)

Blend all ingredients well.

Makes approximately ¾ cup (180 mL)

Handy hint: White wine vinegar may replace white vinegar.

VIRGIN OLIVE OIL
Virgin olive oil is oil taken from the first pressing of the olives, and so tastes especially delicious.

VINAIGRETTE

2 tablespoons white vinegar
1 tablespoon freshly squeezed lemon
** juice**
1 teaspoon prepared mustard
5 tablespoons virgin olive oil

Beat vinegar, lemon juice and mustard together. Add oil, 1 teaspoon at a time, beating well.

Makes approximately ¾ cup (180 mL)

TASTY VARIATION:
☐ Add 1 tablespoon very finely chopped shallots.

BASIC NEW POTATO SALAD

12 new potatoes
1 sprig fresh mint
4 shallots, finely diced
1 tablespoon chopped fresh parsley

Wash new potatoes leaving skins on. Bring to the boil and cook 20 minutes until tender (or microwave, covered, in 1 teaspoon water on HIGH 5–8 minutes, stand for 2 minutes). Stand, when cool, slice or dice potatoes into a salad bowl. Add remaining ingredients and chill.

Delicious with Vinaigrette (see recipe) this salad can also be served with any dressing you prefer.

Serves 6

GREEK SALAD

½ lettuce eg, cos, iceberg or endive
2 radishes, sliced
4 tomatoes, cut into wedges
1 cucumber, sliced
12 black olives
85 g feta cheese
12 anchovy fillets
Basic New Potato Salad (see recipe)

Wash lettuce, shake well and tear into pieces. Use to line a salad bowl. Add all ingredients, crumbling feta cheese, and arrange attractively. Serve with Herb Dressing (see recipe).

Serves 6

HOT POTATO SALAD

2 rashers bacon, diced
2 slices bread, diced
3 tablespoons sour cream
½ cup mayonnaise (125 mL)
2 hardboiled eggs, shelled and sliced
Basic New Potato Salad (see recipe)
grated tasty cheese, to garnish

Fry bacon and bread together until crisp and brown. Drain on kitchen paper towel and place in an ovenproof dish. Add all ingredients and sprinkle with cheese. Heat in 180°C (350°F) oven for 15 minutes (or microwave on HIGH 5 minutes). Serve hot with frankfurts, rissoles or barbecued meat.

Serves 6

Greek Salad, Hot Potato Salad, French Vegetable Salad

POTATO NUT SALAD

2 green apples, cored and diced
2 tablespoons freshly squeezed
lemon juice
Basic New Potato Salad (see recipe)
4 stalks celery, finely diced
½ red capsicum, seeded and diced
4 tablespoons pine nuts or walnuts

Place apple in a salad bowl. To prevent browning sprinkle with lemon juice and stand for 1 minute. Add all remaining ingredients. Serve chilled with your favourite salad dressing (see recipes).

Serves 6

FRENCH VEGETABLE SALAD

3 carrots, scraped and diced
250 g green beans, sliced
250 g green peas
½ small cauliflower, in florets
1 cucumber, diced
pepper, to taste
Basic New Potato Salad (see recipe)

Boil or steam carrots and cauliflower together until just tender, about 10 minutes (or microwave, covered and with 1 teaspoon water on HIGH 5 minutes). Halfway through cooking, add peas and beans. Drain; reserve liquid and store for stock for soup recipes.

Combine vegetables with pepper and basic potato salad in a bowl and chill thoroughly. Serve with your favourite salad dressing (see recipes).

Serves 6

SEAFOOD SALAD

1 squid sac
milk, to soak
500 g uncooked (green) prawns
1 cup water (250 mL)
1 cup white wine (250 mL)
Basic New Potato Salad (see recipe)

Cut squid into thin strips. Place in a bowl, cover with milk and soak for at least 30 minutes. Peel prawns, devein and cut in half.

Combine water and wine in a pan and bring to the boil. Cook prawns until just pink, then remove with a slotted spoon. Transfer to a salad bowl. Add squid to liquid, bring to boil then drain on kitchen paper towel. Add to salad bowl with basic potato salad and chill. Serve with French Dressing or Tasty Mayonnaise (see recipes).

Serves 6

CREAMY SALAD DRESSING

½ cup mayonnaise (125 mL), bought or homemade (see *Tasty Mayonnaise* recipe)
3 tablespoons sour cream
3 tablespoons apple juice
3 egg yolks
2 tablespoons virgin olive oil
1 tablespoon lemon juice

Combine all ingredients in a blender and process until smooth. If mixing by hand, combine all ingredients except oil, beat well and very gradually add oil until blended.

Makes approximately 1¼ cups (310 mL)

TASTY VARIATION:
☐ Replace oil and lemon juice with 3 tablespoons bought Italian dressing;
☐ replace apple juice with 1 peeled, sliced apple.

DILL DRESSING

2 tablespoons white vinegar
½ tablespoon chopped fresh dill
½ cup virgin olive oil (125 mL)

Combine all ingredients in a screw-top jar and shake well.

Makes approximately ¾ cup (180 mL)

SALADE DOLOISE

6 slices ham, diced
100 g green beans, sliced and cooked
2 shallots, diced
2 tomatoes, cut into wedges
Basic Potato Salad (see recipe)
Creamy Salad Dressing (see recipe)

Combine all salad ingredients in a salad bowl. Pour dressing over and chill.

Serves 6

HUANCAINA PAPAS

This is a traditional potato salad from the country which first cultivated potatoes – Peru.

259 g cottage cheese
freshly squeezed lemon juice
Basic Potato Salad (see recipe)
6 lettuce cups
1 teaspoon paprika

Combine cottage cheese and lemon juice. Mix well, then stir with a fork through the potato salad. Serve in lettuce cups sprinkled with paprika.

Serves 6

HERRING POTATO SALAD

lettuce leaves, washed
200 g canned herrings in tomato sauce
Basic Potato Salad (see recipe)
1 pickled cucumber, sliced
Creamy Salad Dressing (see recipe)

Line a salad bowl with lettuce leaves. Break herrings into chunks and place in salad bowl with potato salad and cucumber. Add tomato sauce from herrings to creamy salad dressing and pour over salad. Chill thoroughly and serve.

Serves 6

TASTY VARIATION:
☐ Replace herrings with 250 g sardines or 250 g rollmops.

POTATO AND BEETROOT SALAD WITH DILL DRESSING

225 g canned beetroot, whole or sliced
2 tablespoons chopped fresh chives
Basic Potato Salad (see recipe)
Dill Dressing (see recipe)

Drain beetroot and combine with chives and potato salad in a salad bowl. Serve with dill dressing.

Serves 6

THE NUTRITIOUS POTATO				
EACH 90 g POTATO CONTAINS	BAKED	BOILED	CREAMED (MASHED)	FRIED
Protein	2.1 g	1.5 g	1.7 g	3.6 g
Fat	0.1 g	0.1 g	3.8 g	15 g
Carbohydrate	23 g	18 g	15 g	36 g
Calcium	9.0 mg	7.2 mg	23.4 mg	17.1 mg
Iron	1.2 mg	0.3 mg	0.2 mg	0.7 mg
Sodium	7.2 mg	4.5 mg	265 mg	200.0 mg
Vitamin A	0	0	18	0
Thiamine	0.1 mg	0.1 mg	.07 mg	0.16 mg
Riboflavin	.03 mg	0.02 mg	0.04 mg	0.03 mg
Niacin	1.4 mg	1.2 mg	1.0 mg	3 mg
Ascorbic Acid	11.0 mg	6.3 mg	5.4 mg	9.0 mg
Calories	98	77	95	284

KEY
Gramme – g
Milligramme – mg

PEELING TOMATOES
To peel tomatoes, use a sharp knife to cut out the core. Score the other end with a cross. Cover tomatoes with boiling water for 1 minute, drain and then peel tomatoes.

Delicious Dressings for Potato Salads

Dressings are crucial to any salad. For those who prefer basic dressing, prepare your salad, take it to the table, and just before eating, pour on vinegar and oil, in the ratio of one part vinegar to two parts oil. For those who prefer something a little fancier, the range is endless. Try the following recipes, and experiment by creating your own.

CLASSIC DRESSING

1 tablespoon cold water
yolks from 3 hardboiled eggs
150 mL cream
1 tablespoon white vinegar
¼ teaspoon cayenne pepper

Combine water and egg yolks in a blender. Add cream, vinegar and pepper and blend again. Chill. This mixture will thicken but should be of a pouring consistency.

If mixing by hand, mix egg yolks to a paste with water, then add other ingredients very slowly.

Makes approximately ¾ cup (180 mL)

> **DRIED VERSUS FRESH**
> Dried herbs may be used instead of fresh herbs. Replace with a quarter of the recommended quantity of fresh herbs.
> ½ tablespoon chopped fresh herbs
> = ½ teaspoon dried
> 1 tablespoon chopped fresh herbs
> = 1 teaspoon dried
> 2 tablespoons chopped fresh herbs
> = 2 teaspoons dried

HERB DRESSING

4 shallots, finely diced
1 clove garlic, crushed
1 tablespoon chopped fresh parsley
2 tablespoons chopped fresh basil
1 tablespoon chopped fresh marjoram
1 tablespoon chopped fresh thyme
½ cup virgin olive oil (125 mL)
2 tablespoons white vinegar
½ teaspoon sugar
1 tablespoon freshly squeezed lemon juice

Combine all ingredients and blend well.

Makes approximately 1 cup (250 mL)

TOMATO DRESSING

4 tablespoons tomato sauce
4 tablespoons natural (unflavoured) yoghurt
2 tablespoons virgin olive oil
1 tablespoon freshly squeezed lemon juice

Combine all ingredients and mix well.

Makes approximately 1 cup (250 mL)

Classic Dressing, Herb Dressing and Tomato Dressing

Main Courses

*Potato dishes can make filling, substantial meals.
Crepes, soups, pies, souffles, stews, flans, rolls, pastry
parcels, potatoes with fish, chicken, meat and vegetables
— this selection can feed the family and provide the basis
for many successful dinner parties.*

LUSCIOUS POTATO CREPES

250 g cream cheese
1 tablespoon flour
2 eggs, beaten
1 cup grated tasty cheese (125 g)
**4 potatoes, peeled and grated
    (squeeze out excess moisture)**
pepper, to taste
1 tablespoon chopped fresh parsley
3–6 tablespoons cream or milk
1 tablespoon oil or butter

FILLINGS
1. **6 mushrooms, sauteed;**
2. **3 tablespoons ham, diced or
    chicken cooked and diced,
    1 tablespoon chopped chives
    and 4 tablespoons sour cream;**
3. **125 g chicken livers cooked and
    1 onion, sliced and sauteed;**
4. **2 rashers bacon and 1 tomato,
    chopped and fried together;**
5. **1 green-skinned apple, cored and
    diced mixed with 3 tablespoons
    light blue cheese and
    1 tablespoon chopped walnuts;**
6. **1 cup cooked chopped spinach,
    1 tablespoon pine nuts and
    1 clove garlic, crushed, and all
    fried in 20 g butter**

Mash cream cheese and flour together.
Beat in eggs, cheese, grated potatoes,
pepper and parsley. Add sufficient cream
to make a thick batter.

Heat oil in small frying pan. Pour in 1
tablespoon batter; move pan to spread
batter over base and brown both sides.
To keep crepes warm, stack on a plate,
cover with foil and set over a pan of
simmering water.

Serve crepes with the filling of your
own choice in the centre; and/or serve
with bacon, a salad or as an accompaniment to other dishes.

Serves 6

POTATO OMELETTE

**4 medium potatoes, peeled and
    cooked**
6 eggs, separated
2 onions, grated
1 teaspoon chopped fresh parsley
pepper, to taste
40 g butter

FILLINGS
**2 tablespoons grated tasty cheese
    per omelette *or***
**2 rashers bacon, diced and cooked to
    a crisp *or***
**4 mushrooms, sliced and sauted with
    2 tablespoons grated cheese**

Preheat oven to 140°C (275°F).

Drain and mash potatoes with egg
yolks, onions, parsley and pepper. Whisk
egg whites until stiff and fold into potato
mixture.

Melt butter in a frying pan, swirling to
coat the pan. Pour in one-sixth of the
potato mixture. Gently move mixture
around until just starting to set. Cook until
the omelette sets, then carefully ease
onto a plate using an egg slice.

Place a spoonful of filling on one side
of the omelette and fold over. Place in
oven to keep warm. Repeat until all six
omelettes have been made. Serve with
bacon or salad.

Serves 6

INSTANT GRAVY THICKENER
If your gravy needs thickening, add
a tablespoon or so of mashed
potato.

Luscious Potato Crepes

FISHERMAN'S PIE

700 g white fish fillets (see *Note*)
pepper, to taste
1 cup milk (250 mL)
1 tablespoon lemon juice
20 g butter

SAUCE
60 g butter
2 tablespoons flour
1 cup milk (250 mL)
2 hardboiled eggs, shelled and sliced
3 tablespoons chopped fresh parsley
1 tablespoon capers, drained
110 g prawns, peeled and cooked

TOPPING
4 medium potatoes, cooked and
   mashed
20 g butter
½ cup sour cream (125 mL)
pinch nutmeg

Arrange fish fillets in an ovenproof dish and season with pepper. Pour over milk and lemon juice and dot with butter. Cover and bake at 180°C (350°F) for 15–20 minutes (or microwave on HIGH 8 minutes, using ½ cup of milk only).

Reserve any cooking liquid. Remove any skin and flake fish into large pieces.

To make the sauce, melt butter in a pan and stir in flour. Cook for 1 minute. Remove from heat. Gradually stir in milk and reserved cooking liquid. Return to heat, bring to the boil and thicken, stirring well.

(To microwave sauce, place butter in a jug, microwave on HIGH 1 minute. Add flour and microwave on HIGH 1 minute, gradually stirring in milk and reserved cooking liquid. Microwave on HIGH 3–4 minutes until the mixture boils and thickens.)

Add sliced hardboiled eggs to the sauce together with the fish, parsley, capers and prawns. Spoon back into the ovenproof dish.

To make topping, combine mashed potatoes with butter and sour cream. Pile on top of the fish mixture and sprinkle over a little nutmeg. Return to oven and reheat for approximately 15 minutes (or microwave on HIGH 3 minutes). Serve with salad or cooked vegetables.

Serves 6

Note: Mullet, trevally, snapper or bream fillets, are delicious white fish to use. Also ideal for this recipe, is 700 g of smoked cod or haddock. Cooking the smoked fish in the milk takes away the strong salty flavour.

TASTY VARIATION:
☐ To make a more colourful dish, leave out the prawns, and substitute 2 tomatoes, chopped or ½ cup of cooked peas or sliced carrots (50 g).

1. Pour milk over fish fillets in an ovenproof dish.

2. Flake fish into large pieces.

3. To make sauce, melt butter and stir in flour.

4. To make topping, combine mashed potatoes, butter and sour cream.

5. Pile topping over fish mixture and return to oven.

Meaty Potato Courses

On the following two pages, you will find some well-known recipes which feature both meat and potatoes. These hearty dishes are particularly suitable for cold winter nights, dinner parties or extra-hungry teenagers.

CORNISH PASTIES

250 g round steak, trimmed and diced
2 medium potatoes, peeled and diced
2 tablespoons chopped fresh parsley
2 carrots, scraped and diced
2 onions, diced
2 tablespoons fresh peas
3 tablespoons water
1 beef stock cube
2 tablespoons tomato sauce
2 tablespoons flour
double quantity Flan Pastry (see recipe)
1 egg yolk
1 tablespoon milk

In a pan, combine meat, potatoes, parsley, carrots, onions, peas, water and stock cube and bring to the boil. Simmer 10 minutes then remove from heat and cool thoroughly. Drain, reserving liquid to mix with tomato sauce and flour to make gravy.

Preheat oven to 250°C (475°F). Cut pastry into three portions. Roll out one portion into a square and cut in half. Mix egg yolk and milk together and brush over all pastry edges to glaze. Place one-sixth of vegetable mixture in centre of each half, and fold to form a triangle. Press edges together with fingers, making a 'frilled' edge. Place on a greased tray.

Repeat with remaining pastry and filling. Brush all triangles with remaining egg-milk mixture and bake approximately 30 minutes until crisp and brown. While baking, make gravy. Combine reserved liquid, tomato sauce and flour and bring to the boil, stirring until gravy thickens (or microwave on HIGH 3 minutes or until gravy boils and thickens). Serve hot with pasties.

Makes 6

Note: Uncooked, prepared pasties can be frozen for up to three months. Allow an extra 5 minutes cooking time.

FLAN PASTRY

1 cup flour (125 g)
pinch salt
60 g butter
1 egg yolk
squeeze lemon juice
cold water
1 egg beaten with 2 tablespoons milk, to glaze (if baking blind)

Place flour and salt in a bowl. With fingertips only, mix butter to a breadcrumb consistency. Mix in egg yolk and lemon juice. With a knife 'cut' in 1 tablespoon water, adding a little more if necessary to form a stiff dough.

Turn out onto a floured board and knead gently into a smooth ball. If using to make a flan, roll out to size of flan dish and line dish. Prick base with a fork. If baking blind, glaze flan with egg and milk then prick base. Cook in a 180°C (350°F) oven for 15–20 minutes or until golden brown.

Makes 1 x 20 cm flan

STORING PASTRY CASES
The cooked flan base will store for 5 days in an airtight container. When making it, make double the quantity. Freeze half. Pastry, either cooked or uncooked can be frozen for up to 3 months.

---

3. Spoon one sixth of filling onto each

1. Cut pastry into three portions.

2. Roll out each portion and cut in half.

LAMB NAVARIN WITH NEW POTATOES

500 g lamb stewing chops
20 g butter
2 onions, diced
1 clove garlic, crushed
3 carrots, scraped and diced
4 tablespoons flour
1 tablespoon tomato paste
pinch dried thyme
1 bay leaf
pepper, to taste
470 mL canned beef consomme
½ cup water (125 mL)
6 new potatoes, washed
2 tablespoons chopped fresh parsley

Arrange chops in an ovenproof casserole dish.

Melt butter in a pan, add onions and fry until transparent, then add garlic and carrots. Add flour, tomato paste, thyme, bay leaf, pepper, beef consomme and water. Stir until smooth. Bring to the boil then pour over chops. Add potatoes and parsley. Bake, covered at 180°C (350°F) for 1½ hours.

Serves 6

BEEF BOURGUIGNON

1 kg topside beef
flour, for coating
20 g butter
1 clove garlic, crushed
2 rashers bacon, diced
1 beef stock cube
6–8 small new potatoes, washed
6–8 small onions, peeled
pinch dried thyme
1 bay leaf
½ cup water (125 mL)
½ cup red wine (125 mL)
3 tablespoons brandy

Trim fat off meat. Cut meat into cubes and toss in flour to coat. Melt butter, add garlic and bacon and lightly fry. Add meat and brown.

Transfer to a casserole dish. Crumble stock cube over meat and add all remaining ingredients.

Cover and cook in the oven at 180°C (350°F) for 1½ hours.

Serve hot with green vegetables, or a green salad.

Serves 6

TASTY VARIATION:
☐ Add 125 g small mushrooms 20 minutes before the dish has completed cooking.

POTATOES WITH BEEF 'N' BEER

500 g topside beef
25 g packet French onion soup mix
2 potatoes, peeled and diced
1½ cups beer (375 mL)
1 French breadstick
French mustard
grated tasty cheese, to sprinkle

Trim fat off beef. Cut beef into cubes and toss in the onion soup mixture to coat. In a pan, combine beef, potatoes and beer and bring to the boil. Simmer 1½ hours.

When cooked, spoon into six individual bowls. Cut breadstick into six thick slices, spread with French mustard and place a slice on top of meat in each ramekin, mustard side down.

Top with grated tasty cheese and brown under griller (or microwave on HIGH until the cheese melts and bubbles). Serve as a complete dish or accompanied by green vegetables or salad.

Serves 6

TASTY VARIATION:
☐ 1 cup (100 g) sliced vegetables e.g. peas or carrots, can be added and cooked with the meat.

POTATO FLAN

40 g butter
1 onion, sliced
1 clove garlic, crushed
2 medium potatoes, peeled and grated
3 eggs
2 tablespoons diced ham
2 tablespoons grated tasty cheese
1 tablespoon chopped fresh parsley
1 tablespoon chopped fresh chives
185 g ready-rolled shortcrust pastry or 1 quantity Flan Pastry (see recipe)

Melt butter, add onion and garlic and fry until transparent (or microwave on HIGH 2 minutes). Add grated potatoes. Whisk eggs and add with ham, cheese, parsley, chives to potato-onion mixture. Pour into prepared pastry flan and bake in the oven at 180°C (350°F) for 1 hour. Serve with salad.

Serves 6

TASTY VARIATION:
☐ Replace ham with 2 tablespoons chopped mushrooms, add to onion and saute.

CURRIED MEAT BALLS

2 slices bread
½ cup milk (125 mL)
750 g minced steak
2 eggs, beaten
1 onion, diced
pepper, to taste
1 tablespoon curry powder
4 potatoes, peeled and diced
2 carrots, scraped and diced
300 mL tomato puree
pinch cayenne pepper
pinch ground cumin
pinch ground coriander

Cut crusts from bread and discard (see *Note*). Place bread in a bowl, cover with milk and soak for 5 minutes. Combine minced steak, eggs, onion, pepper and half the curry powder. Squeeze the milk from the bread and add bread to mince mixture. Roll mixture into small balls and chill.

Cook potatoes and carrots in a pan with a little water for 10 minutes (or microwave, covered and with 2 teaspoons water on HIGH 5 minutes). Stir in tomato puree, remaining curry powder, cayenne pepper, cumin, coriander and meat balls and simmer for 30 minutes (or microwave on HIGH 5 minutes, on MEDIUM 8 minutes. Stand for 4 minutes). Serve with boiled rice.

Serves 6

Note: Cut crusts into cubes and bake in a 180°C (350°F) oven until crisp and brown. Use as croutons for soup.

TASTY VARIATIONS:
☐ Substitute beef with pork/veal mince, and/or;
☐ substitute cayenne, cumin and coriander with 1 tablespoon of garam masala.

WATERY BOILED POTATOES
If your boiled potatoes taste too watery, add a little powdered milk.

FULLER FLAVOUR
Cook a casserole 24 hours before serving, as it develops a much richer flavour.

Split Pea and Potato Soup, and Minestrone

CAULIFLOWER SOUP

1 small cauliflower, broken into florets
1 onion, sliced
3 medium potatoes, peeled and sliced
1 chicken stock cube
2 cups water (500 mL)
grated tasty cheese, to sprinkle

In a pan, combine cauliflower florets, onion, potatoes, stock cube and water. Bring to the boil and simmer until vegetables are really tender, about 30 minutes. Blend until smooth or mash well and push through a sieve.

To serve, reheat and spoon into soup bowls (or microwave on HIGH 2 minutes per bowl). Sprinkle with cheese.

Serves 4–6 (depending on size of cauliflower)

CORN AND POTATO SOUP

20 g butter
2 onions, sliced
4 medium potatoes, peeled and sliced
3 cups water (750 mL)
2 chicken stock cubes
½ cup cream (125 mL)
440 g canned creamed corn
1 tablespoon chopped fresh chives, to serve

Melt butter in a pan, add onion and gently fry until transparent. Add potatoes, water and stock cubes and bring to the boil. Lower heat and simmer for 30 minutes. Blend or push through a sieve until smooth. Return to the pan and add cream and corn. Reheat but do not boil. (Alternatively, add cream and corn and microwave on MEDIUM for 4 minutes.)

Serve in soup bowls sprinkled with chives.

Serves 6

TASTY VARIATIONS:
☐ Replace chives with 2 teaspoons nutmeg, or 2 tablespoons grated tasty cheese;
☐ add 3 stalks celery, diced, to the blended soup, before serving.

MINESTRONE

4 rashers bacon, rinds removed and diced
1 onion, diced
1½ bunches fresh parsley, chopped
1 clove garlic, crushed
1 stalk celery, diced
2 medium potatoes, peeled and diced
2 carrots, scraped and diced
1 zucchini, diced
125 g green beans, peeled and chopped
310 g canned red kidney beans, drained
3 tomatoes, peeled and chopped
1.5 litres water
1 cup uncooked white rice (185 g), optional
100 g cabbage, shredded
grated Parmesan cheese, to serve
crusty bread, to serve

Combine diced bacon and onion in a pan and fry for 1 minute. Add all the vegetables except cabbage and cover with water. Bring to the boil and simmer for 1 hour. If using white rice, add and cook a further 30 minutes. Add cabbage and simmer another 30 minutes. Serve in a tureen together with a bowl of Parmesan cheese and crusty bread.

Serves 6

SPLIT PEA AND POTATO SOUP

500 g dried peas
1.5 litres water
500 g bacon bones
3 large potatoes, peeled and sliced
2 onions, sliced
2 stalks celery, diced
1 cup milk (250 mL)
croutons or finely diced, cooked bacon, to serve

Soak dried peas overnight in 3 cups water (750 mL).

Next day strain and discard the water. Place 3 cups water (750 mL) in a pan with bacon bones and simmer for 1 hour. Add peas, potatoes, onions and celery and simmer for a further hour. Remove bones and scrape off meat. Discard bones and return meat to the soup.

Blend till smooth or mash well and push through a sieve. Add sufficient milk to reach the thickness you prefer. Reheat (or microwave on HIGH 5 minutes).

Serve with croutons or bacon.

Serves 6

TASTY VARIATION:
☐ Add 1 carrot, diced, to the vegetables when cooking.

POTATOES AND SILVERBEET WITH FETTUCCINE

200 g red potatoes, peeled and
    cut into 1 cm diced pieces
1 small bunch silverbeet, rinsed,
    leaves and stalks separated
80 g butter
3 cloves garlic, crushed
1 Spanish onion, coarsely chopped
1 tablespoon finely chopped fresh
    sage, oregano or parsley
½ red capsicum, julienned
500 g fresh wholemeal fettuccine
    or 350 g dried
125 g grated fontina cheese
30 g grated Parmesan cheese
salt and pepper, to taste

In a saucepan of boiling salted water, boil potatoes until tender but crisp for 3–4 minutes; remove with a slotted spoon and set aside.

Slice silverbeet stalks into 1 cm pieces. Slice leaves into thin strips and place in a large colander.

In the saucepan of boiling water cook silverbeet stalks for 5–6 minutes. Now pour the contents of the saucepan, (including the water) over the beet leaves in the colander. Turn over with a wooden spoon and leave to drain and cool in the sink.

Melt butter in a large frying pan and gently saute garlic, onion and herbs for 5–6 minutes. Do not brown the onion, only soften it. Add potatoes, beet stalks and leaves and capsicum and toss lightly. Cover and cook for 5 minutes.

Cook and drain fettuccine and transfer to a large buttered shallow ovenproof dish. Add the silverbeet mixture and toss to combine. Add cheeses, season and toss again.

Cover and bake at 190°C (375°F) for 20 minutes, or until cheeses are melted through and bubbling.

Serves 4

BAKED TORTELLINI

250 g eggplant
salt
200 g tortellini, filled with beef
    or cheese
250 g potatoes, peeled and cut into
    2 cm thick slices
½ cup olive oil (125 mL)
1 onion, sliced thinly
400 g canned Italian peeled tomatoes
½ teaspoon chopped fresh oregano
pinch cayenne pepper
salt and pepper, to taste
100 g shredded fontina cheese
2 tablespoons extra chopped fresh
    oregano or parsley

Dice eggplant into 2 cm pieces, sprinkle with salt and leave to drain over the sink in a colander or strainer.

Boil tortellini and when cooked drain and place in a shallow ovenproof dish.

In a small saucepan, boil potatoes until just cooked; drain. Heat some oil in a frying pan and saute potatoes until brown, then add to the tortellini.

With a little more oil, saute onion gently for 5 minutes and then add drained eggplant. Continue cooking, adding more oil if necessary, until the eggplant is tender and golden.

Drain tomatoes and add to the pan, breaking them up with a wooden spoon while stirring in. Add seasonings and cook for a further 5–8 minutes, or until the tomatoes have reduced and there is a little liquid left.

Add to the dish with tortellini and toss through with one-third of the fontina. Distribute remaining fontina over the top and sprinkle with the extra fresh oregano or parsley.

Bake at 190°C (375°F) for 10 minutes so that the cheese melts through and bubbles on top.

Serves 4

Baked Tortellini, Potatoes and Silverbeet with Fettuccine

SALMON ROLLS

6 whole cabbage leaves (or outer leaves of lettuce)
2 carrots, grated
440 g canned red salmon, drained
4 medium potatoes, cooked and mashed
2 tablespoons mayonnaise
2 cups water (500 mL)
2 tablespoons tomato paste
1 chicken stock cube
1 tablespoon cornflour mixed with 2 tablespoons water
crusty bread, to serve

Remove any thick stalks from the cabbage. Place leaves in a pan carefully to avoid breaking them. Cover with water and bring to the boil. Remove from heat and stand 3 minutes (or microwave on HIGH 2 minutes; allow to cool before removing from microwave). Drain and pat dry.

Combine grated carrots with salmon, potatoes and mayonnaise. Spoon equal quantities into the centre of each cabbage leaf and roll carefully, tucking the ends under. Arrange in an ovenproof dish in a single layer.

Combine water, tomato paste and crumbled stock cube and pour over salmon rolls. Bake uncovered in the oven at 180°C (350°F) for 45 minutes (or microwave on HIGH 15 minutes using only 1 cup water mixed with tomato paste and stock cube).

Remove rolls, set aside and keep warm. Pour stock into a pan and mix in cornflour paste. Stir over heat until the mixture boils and thickens (or microwave on HIGH 2 minutes).

Cut salmon rolls in half. Place two halves on each plate and spoon over some of the thickened stock. Serve with crusty warm bread.

Serves 6

TASTY VARIATION:
☐ Replace salmon with 200 g cooked, diced chicken.

SHORTCUTS
4 tablespoons of instant potato mixed with hot water is a quick replacement for 2 medium potatoes, cooked.

FISH PARCELS

20 g butter
1 onion, sliced
2 potatoes, peeled and thinly sliced
2 tomatoes, sliced
1 capsicum, seeded and sliced
6 fresh fish fillets or cutlets
oil
2 tablespoons lemon juice
3 tablespoons white wine
1 tablespoon chopped fresh chives
1 tablespoon cornflour mixed with 2 tablespoons water

Melt butter, add onion and fry until transparent (or microwave together on HIGH 2 minutes). Add potatoes, tomatoes and capsicum and stir for 1 minute (or microwave on HIGH 45 seconds).

Lightly oil six pieces of aluminium foil (or microwave wrap). Place a piece of fish on each piece of foil and spoon mixed vegetables on top. Sprinkle with lemon juice, wine and chives. Fold foil around fish mixture making a parcel.

Arrange in a baking dish and bake at 180°C (350°F) for 30 minutes (or microwave on HIGH 8–10 minutes, checking to see when fish is cooked). Carefully make a small hole in the bags and pour off liquid into a pan. Stir cornflour paste into fish juices and heat until sauce thickens (or combine fish juices and cornflour paste and microwave on HIGH 2 minutes.)

To serve, carefully unwrap fish, slide onto plates and pour sauce over.

Serves 6

TASTY VARIATION:
☐ Replace fish with 6 chump chops, trimmed of fat and cook with vegetables in 180°C (350°F) oven 45 minutes.

MEAT LOAF WITH TASTY TOMATO TOPPING

2 medium potatoes, cooked and dry mashed
500 g minced steak
1 egg
25 g packet French onion soup mix
1 cup milk (250 mL)

TOPPING
3 tablespoons tomato sauce
pinch dry mustard
1 tablespoon brown sugar

Combine potatoes, steak, egg, French onion soup mix and milk. Mix well and spoon into a meatloaf tin.

Combine topping ingredients and spread over the top of the meatloaf. Bake at 180°C (350°F) for 1 hour (or microwave on HIGH 25 minutes. Stand for 5 minutes before serving).

Serve hot with vegetables, or cold with a salad. This recipe is also great to freeze and serve in an emergency.

Serves 6

TASTY VARIATIONS:
☐ 500 g mixture of lamb mince and pork mince; or
☐ three pineapple slices placed on the topping, then baked.

SEMOLINA GNOCCHI WITH VEAL AND TOMATO SAUCE

GNOCHHI
3 medium potatoes, cooked and dry mashed
1½ cups milk (375 mL)
100 g fine semolina
1 teaspoon nutmeg
2 eggs, beaten

VEAL AND TOMATO SAUCE
40 g butter
1 onion, sliced
2 cloves garlic, crushed
500 g minced veal
470 g canned tomatoes, drained and liquid reserved
2 tablespoons tomato paste
2 cups white wine (500 mL)
1 cup water (250 mL)
2 chicken stock cubes
1 teaspoon sugar
1 teaspoon fresh basil leaves
grated Parmesan cheese, and 2 tablespoons chopped fresh parsley, to garnish

In a pan, combine mashed potatoes and milk. Bring to simmering point. Add semolina and nutmeg and stir until mixture becomes thick and very stiff. Remove from heat and beat in eggs. Spoon into a greased casserole dish and leave overnight. When ready, cut into squares and cook in boiling water. Boil for 1 minute after gnocchi rise to the top of pan, then remove with a slotted spoon. Drain on kitchen paper towels and set aside to keep warm.

To make sauce, melt butter in a pan, add onion and fry until transparent (or microwave butter and onion on HIGH 2 minutes). Stir in remaining ingredients (including liquid from tomatoes) and bring to the boil. Simmer 1½ hours uncovered.

Pour sauce over gnocchi and garnish with a sprinkle of Parmesan cheese and fresh parsley.

Serves 4–6

FISH A LA GREQUE

2 potatoes, peeled and sliced
2 onions, sliced
250 g fresh fish fillets
2 tomatoes, sliced
1 tablespoon safflower oil
½ cup water (125 mL)
pepper, to taste
2 tablespoons chopped fresh parsley

Grease a casserole dish. Arrange potatoes and onions on base, with fish fillets on top. Cover with sliced tomatoes.

Mix together oil, water, pepper and parsley and pour over casserole. Bake at 180°C (350°F) for 30 minutes (or microwave on HIGH 8 minutes). Serve with a salad and fresh bread.

Serves 6

TASTY VARIATION:
☐ Replace fresh tomatoes with 440 g canned tomatoes, sliced, and use tomato liquid in place of water.

SAUTEED POTATOES WITH CHICKEN AND MUSHROOMS

Although this dish is made with chicken it is delicious with any leftover cooked meat.

3 medium potatoes, peeled, sliced and cooked
1 tablespoon oil
pepper, to taste
20 g butter
1 onion, peeled and sliced
110 g mushrooms, sliced
250 g cooked chicken meat
½ cup cream (125 mL)
1 tablespoon sherry
pinch paprika

Drain the potatoes and carefully pat dry with kitchen paper towel.

In a frying pan heat oil and fry potatoes until golden brown. Season and remove with a slotted spoon. Keep hot in the oven at 180°C (350°F), (or microwave on HIGH 2 minutes when ready to use).

In the same pan, melt butter and fry onion until transparent. Stir in mushrooms and cook a further 1 minute. Add chicken meat and continue stirring for 4 minutes (or microwave butter and onion on HIGH 2 minutes, add mushrooms and chicken meat and cook on HIGH 2 minutes).

Add cream and sherry, bring to the boil and simmer 5 minutes (or microwave cream and sherry on MEDIUM 2 minutes). To serve, spoon vegetable/chicken mixture onto a large warmed serving dish and surround with potatoes. Sprinkle with paprika.

Serves 6

Fish a la Greque, Sauteed Potatoes with Chicken and Mushrooms, and Semolina Gnocchi with Veal and Tomato Sauce

POTATO SOUFFLE WITH TANGY BACON SAUCE

3 medium potatoes, peeled and cooked
20 g butter
4 tablespoons sour cream
1 tablespoon chopped fresh chives
pepper, to taste
4 eggs, separated
125 g grated tasty cheese

TANGY BACON SAUCE
20 g butter
4 rashers bacon, rind removed and diced
3 tablespoons tomato sauce
1 tablespoon Worcestershire sauce
2 tablespoons water
2 chicken stock cubes

Mash potatoes until smooth with butter, sour cream, chives, pepper, yolks and cheese. Whisk egg whites until stiff. Carefully fold into potato mixture. Spoon into a greased souffle dish, running a knife in a circle 2.5 cm deep into the centre of the mixture. (This will, when cooked, form a raised top). Stand in a dish of warm water and bake at 180°C (350°F) for 45 minutes, or until a knife inserted in the side of the souffle comes out clean. Serve immediately with sauce.

To make sauce, melt butter, add bacon and gently fry until crisp (or microwave butter and bacon, covered, on HIGH, 4 minutes).

Stir in other ingredients and bring to the boil, stirring well (or microwave other ingredients on HIGH 2 minutes). Serve hot.

Serves 6

TASTY VARIATIONS:
Add to the potato mixture any of the following:
☐ 2 tablespoons corn and ½ capsicum finely diced;
☐ 2 tablespoons, bacon diced and cooked and 1 onion, diced and fried.

POTATO PANCAKES WITH SOUR CREAM AND APPLE SAUCE

3 large potatoes , peeled and grated
6 shallots, finely chopped
2 eggs, beaten
4 tablespoons dried breadcrumbs
butter and oil
sour cream, to serve

APPLE SAUCE
500 g cooking apples, peeled, cored and sliced
3 tablespoons sugar

Squeeze moisture from grated potatoes. Combine in a bowl with shallots, eggs, and breadcrumbs.

In a heavy-based pan, melt equal quantities of butter and oil, about 1 tablespoon of each at a time. Drop in spoonfuls of potato mixture, fry and flip over. Cook until golden on both sides.

To make apple sauce, cook sliced apples in a saucepan with enough water to avoid burning them, until apples form a soft pulp. Add sugar, stir to dissolve and serve with pancakes and sour cream.

Serves 4

OMELETTE WITH CRISPY PAN-FRIED POTATOES

Ideally use two pans, one for the omelette and the other for the filling. If using only one pan cook the filling first, set aside keeping warm then cook the omelette.

4 medium potatoes, peeled and diced
3 tablespoons oil
4 rashers bacon, rind removed and diced
1 onion, peeled and diced
8 button mushrooms washed and sliced

OMELETTE
12 eggs (allow 2 per person)
pepper, to taste
120 g butter

Boil potatoes until tender (or microwave potatoes, covered and with 1 teaspoon water, on HIGH 8 minutes). Heat oil, add bacon and onion and gently fry until onion is transparent. Add mushrooms and stir 2 minutes. Remove all ingredients with a slotted spoon and drain on kitchen paper towel.

Place cooked potatoes in pan and stir until brown. If potatoes start to stick add a little more oil. Return other ingredients to pan and stir until heated through. Divide potato mixture into sixths.

Preheat oven to 140°C (275°F).

To make omelette beat 2 eggs lightly and season with pepper. Melt 20 g butter in the pan. Add eggs as butter begins to froth — don't allow the butter to brown. Swirl eggs around the pan, forking them into the centre so the remaining liquid can run into the spaces and cook through. Continue until the eggs have set underneath but are still moist on top. Carefully ease omelette onto a warmed plate. Spoon one-sixth of potato mixture onto omelette and fold over. Place in oven to keep warm. Repeat until all six omelettes have been made.

Serves 6

FINNISH PIE

60 g dried mushrooms (see Glossary)
40 g butter
1 onion, sliced
1 rasher bacon, diced
1 kg fresh field mushrooms, washed and sliced
pepper, to taste
2 tablespoons cream
½ cup dried breadcrumbs (60 g)

PUREE
4 medium potatoes, cooked
1 cup hot milk (250 mL)
1 egg, beaten
20 g butter

Soak dried mushrooms in hot water for 10 minutes; drain, squeeze dry and chop finely. Melt butter in a pan and fry onion and bacon until bacon is crisp (or microwave butter, onion and bacon on HIGH 3 minutes). Add all the mushrooms and pepper and fry for 2 minutes (or microwave mushrooms and pepper on HIGH 2 minutes). Stir in cream.

Mash potatoes with hot milk, then beat in egg and butter to form a puree.

Grease a shallow dish and pour in half the potato puree, spoon over the mushroom mixture and top with remaining puree. Sprinkle top with breadcrumbs and dot with butter. Bake in the oven at 180°C (350°F) for 20 minutes (or microwave on HIGH 4 minutes). Serve with sweet and sour cucumber (see *Note*) or a green salad.

Serves 6

Note: Sweet and sour cucumbers or sliced pickled cucumbers are available from delicatessens and some supermarkets.

TASTY VARIATION:
☐ Replace mushrooms and bacon with 12 fresh scallops. Cover the scallops with cream and allow to stand for 20 minutes. This makes the scallops juicy and plump. Use the cream in the sauce.

Potato Pancakes with Sour Cream and Apple Sauce

Classic Accompaniments

In many countries, potatoes are served with a main meal at least once a day. The French, in particular, have adopted the potato as their own, and to them we owe many of the superb dishes found in restaurants around the world. Some of our recipes make serving suggestions, but you can enjoy them with almost anything.

POTATOES ANNA

6 large potatoes, peeled, washed and thinly sliced
250 g butter

Thickly grease six small custard cups or moulds with butter. Arrange a layer of potatoes on base of each custard cup, top with a small piece of butter. Repeat, reversing the circle. Allow 40 g of butter per cup. Continue, reversing each time, until all the cups are filled.

Stand cups in 1.5 centimetres of hot water in a baking dish. Cover cups with foil. Bake at 180°C (350°F) for 1 hour or until potatoes are tender. (Alternatively, cover with microwave wrap and microwave on HIGH 5 minutes, then MEDIUM 10 minutes or until tender.)

Gently tilt each cup to pour off excess butter. Place a dinner plate on top of the cup and turn upside down. Carefully lift cup from potatoes.

Serves 6

POTATOES ROMANOFF

6 medium potatoes, peeled
6 shallots, finely sliced
160 g grated tasty cheese
300 mL sour cream
1 cup milk (250 mL)
pepper, to taste
½ teaspoon nutmeg

Cut potatoes in half, and cook in boiling water until firm but tender (or microwave whole potatoes on HIGH 8 minutes). Allow to cool.

Coarsely grate potatoes into a greased casserole dish. Add shallots and half the cheese. Combine cream, milk and pepper. Pour over potato and cheese, then top with remaining cheese and the nutmeg.

Chill for 2 hours or overnight. Bake uncovered in the oven at 180°C (350°F) for 40 minutes.

Serves 6

DUCHESSE POTATOES

6 large potatoes, cooked and sliced
2 egg yolks
80 g butter
pinch nutmeg
1 egg, beaten

Mash potatoes with egg yolks, butter and nutmeg. Push mixture through a sieve into an icing bag fitted with a star nozzle. Pipe potatoes onto a greased oven tray, forming medium-sized stars.

Brush with beaten egg and bake in the oven at 180°C (350°F) until golden.

Serves 6

LYONNAISE POTATOES

80 g butter
4 large potatoes, peeled and thinly sliced
2 onions, thinly sliced

Melt 40 g butter in a pan add potatoes, turning until tender and golden brown. While potatoes are cooking, in a separate pan, melt remaining butter and fry onions until tender. To serve, combine and accompany with grilled meats.

Serves 6

Potatoes Romanoff, Lyonnaise Potatoes

Cheesy Potato Fans served with a rack of lamb

SUGAR-GLAZED POTATOES

12 small new potatoes, washed
3 tablespoons white sugar
40 g butter

Boil potatoes until tender (or prick and microwave on HIGH 8 minutes in a covered dish). Drain and chill thoroughly.

Dissolve sugar in a heavy pan, add butter and stir to combine. Add potatoes and stir until browned. Serve immediately.

Serves 6

Handy hints: Cook potatoes the day before and store in refrigerator to chill overnight.

DRY ROASTED POTATOES

6 potatoes, peeled and cut in half lengthways

Place potatoes on an oven rack and dry roast for 30 minutes in the oven at 200°C (400°F).

Serves 6

HONEYED ROAST POTATOES

2 medium potatoes, peeled
2 tablespoons oil
60 g butter
salt, optional
¼ cup honey (90 g)

Add potatoes to a pan of cold water, bring to the boil then drain immediately.

Place potatoes in a baking dish with oil and butter and sprinkle with a little salt (see *Note*).

Bake at 180°C (350°F) for 20 minutes. Baste with honey and bake a further 20 minutes. Serve with any roast meat.

Serves 2

Note: Sprinkling potatoes with a little salt gives a light, crunchy crust. But only small amounts of salt are necessary.

CHEESY POTATO FANS

6 large potatoes, peeled
oil
80 g grated tasty cheese
20 g butter

Cut a small slice from the end of each potato to make a flat base. Place potato, base down, on a large spoon and make a cut 2 cm deep or until the knife touches the edge of the spoon. Repeat with each potato.

Stand potatoes completely covered in cold water for 30 minutes, then drain and pat dry. Just cover the bottom of a baking dish with oil and brush each potato with oil. Stand potatoes in dish and bake at 180°C (350°F) for 1 hour. (This dish is not suitable to microwave.)

Sprinkle with cheese, dot with butter and bake a further 10 minutes.

Serves 6

CHOUX POTATOES

40 g butter
½ cup water (125 mL)
½ cup flour (60 g)
3 eggs
4 medium potatoes, cooked and dry mashed
oil, for deep-frying

Bring butter and water to the boil in a pan. Stir in flour and mix in well until mixture leaves the side of the pan. Remove from heat and cool.

Place in a bowl and add eggs one at a time, beating well with an electric mixer. Stir in mashed potato.

Heat the oil in a frying pan. Drop one tablespoonful of mixture in oil at a time. Fry until golden brown and drain on kitchen paper towels. Serve with any meat or poultry.

Serves 6

TASTY VARIATIONS:
Add any of the following:
☐ ½ cup grated tasty cheese (60 g);
☐ ½ cup canned corn kernels, drained (125 g);
☐ 2 rashers bacon, diced and fried.

POTATOES SMITANA

12 small new potatoes, lightly scrubbed
1 tablespoon oil
40 g butter
1 medium onion, diced
300 mL cream
pepper, to taste
juice 1 lemon
1 tablespoon chopped fresh parsley, to garnish

Add potatoes to boiling water and simmer until tender (or prick potatoes with a fork, place in a covered dish and microwave on HIGH 8 minutes; stand 2 minutes). Drain and keep warm.

Heat oil and butter in a pan. Add onion and gently fry until transparent. Stir in cream and pepper, bring to boil and simmer for 5 minutes. Remove from heat and add lemon juice. Pour cream mixture over potatoes and sprinkle with parsley.

Serves 4

TASTY VARIATION:
☐ Replace lemon juice with 2 tablespoons of sour cream or mayonnaise.

Sauteed Potatoes in Lemon and Garlic served with fish

FRENCH POTATO BALLS

4 medium potatoes, peeled, sliced and cooked
2 tablespoons mayonnaise
1 teaspoon French mustard
1 clove garlic, crushed
1 tablespoon chopped fresh parsley
1 tablespoon chopped fresh chives
pepper, to taste
self-raising flour
2 eggs, beaten with 3 tablespoons water
1½–2 cups dried breadcrumbs (180 g)
oil, for deep-frying

Mash potatoes with mayonnaise, mustard, garlic, parsley, chives, pepper and sufficient flour to make a firm dough.

Roll potato mixture into balls. Dip each ball into the egg-water mix, then roll in breadcrumbs.

Refrigerate coated balls for at least 1 hour. To cook, heat oil and deep-fry balls until brown. Serve with your favourite meal.

Serves 6

Handy hint: When coating food to be fried, always use egg and water, not egg and milk, as milk tends to make food stick to the pan.

TASTY VARIATIONS:
☐ Add 1 tablespoon grated cheese;
☐ the potato can be rolled into balls, chilled and fried without the egg and breadcrumb coating.

SAUTEED POTATOES IN LEMON AND GARLIC

4 large potatoes, peeled
2 tablespoons oil
60 g butter
grated rind 1 lemon
juice 1 lemon
2 tablespoons chopped fresh parsley
3 cloves garlic, crushed

Cut potatoes into 0.5 cm thick slices. Cook in boiling water for 4 minutes (or cover with microwave wrap and microwave with 1 teaspoon water on HIGH 2 minutes). Drain carefully and pat dry with kitchen paper towel.

Heat oil and 40 g butter in a heavy-based pan. Add enough potatoes to cover base of pan and cook, shaking pan so potatoes do not stick. When brown, carefully remove from pan and repeat until all are browned (if necessary add a little more oil and butter).

Combine remaining butter, lemon rind and juice, parsley and garlic in a pan and heat until butter turns a pale brown. Add potatoes and toss until potatoes are well coated.

Serves 4

OIL AND BUTTER
Mixing oil and butter together prevents the butter from burning and removes the oily taste.

DAUPHINOISE POTATOES

20 g butter
1 clove garlic, crushed
4 large potatoes, peeled and sliced
1 egg, beaten
3 cups hot milk (750 mL)
160 g Gruyere cheese, grated
pinch nutmeg

Combine butter and garlic and use to grease a casserole dish. Place sliced potatoes in dish. Mix egg, milk and cheese together, and pour over potatoes. Sprinkle with nutmeg. Bake in the oven at 180°C (350°F) for 1¼ hours or until tender. Serve with roasts or barbequed meats.

Serves 6

TASTY VARIATIONS:
☐ Omit cheese and use only 2 cups milk (500 mL) and 1 cup cream (250 mL);
☐ omit cheese and milk and use 3 cups beef stock (750 mL) instead;
☐ place 4 rashers bacon, diced and cooked on top of potato;
☐ add 1 tablespoon diced fresh chives, and top with ½ cup fresh breadcrumbs (30 g);
☐ in a pan combine 2 tomatoes, sliced, 1 onion, sliced, 1 tablespoon oil, 1 clove garlic, crushed, and ½ teaspoon sugar. Fry until tender. Add to egg-milk mixture and pour over potatoes;
☐ mash together canned anchovies with ½ teaspoon each chopped fresh thyme and basil. Add to the egg-milk mixture and pour over potatoes.

1. Combine butter and garlic.

2. Use garlic butter to grease a casserole dish.

3. Layer sliced potatoes in dish.

4. Mix egg, milk and cheese together in a bowl.

5. Pour over potatoes, sprinkle with nutmeg and bake in the oven.

SPANISH OMELETTE

3 tablespoons olive oil
1 large potato, peeled and diced small
1 large Spanish onion, finely chopped
5 eggs
freshly ground black pepper

Heat oil in a large frying pan. Saute potato and onion, stirring occasionally, until both are cooked but not brown. Whisk eggs with pepper and pour into the pan, spreading evenly. Cover pan, lower heat and allow omelette to cook for about 10 minutes.

Place a plate of a similar size to your frying pan over the top of it and invert the omelette. Return it immediately to the pan and brown the other side.

Serves 4

POTATO KUGEL

20 g butter
4 medium potatoes, cooked and dry mashed
4 eggs, beaten
¼ cup potato flour or cornflour (30 g)
½ teaspoon baking powder
1 small onion, diced pepper
pepper, to taste

Melt butter (or microwave on HIGH 30 seconds) to grease a shallow casserole dish. Combine potatoes and eggs and beat until smooth. Add remaining ingredients and mix well.

Spoon mixture into casserole dish and bake at 180°C (350°F) for 30–35 minutes (or microwave on HIGH 3 minutes, then MEDIUM 8 minutes). Tastes delicious with grilled pork and mushrooms.

Serves 6

TASTY VARIATION:
☐ Add 2 tablespoons grated cheese sprinkled on top of cooked Kugel and brown under griller or in oven.

NOMAD POTATOES

4 large potatoes, peeled and thinly sliced
125 g cream cheese
½ cup milk (125 mL)
1 clove garlic, crushed
2 tablespoons Parmesan cheese
1 tablespoon chopped fresh chives

Boil potatoes carefully until tender (or arrange in a dish with 1 teaspoon water, cover with microwave wrap and microwave on HIGH 7 minutes; stand 2 minutes). Grease a shallow casserole dish and spoon in potatoes.

Beat cream cheese and milk together. Add garlic, pour over potatoes and sprinkle with Parmesan cheese and chives. Bake at 180°C (350°F) for 15 minutes.

Serves 6

TASTY VARIATIONS:
☐ Replace cream cheese with 125 g cottage cheese;
☐ replace Parmesan cheese with 2 tablespoons grated cheddar.

DRY MASHED
Dry mashed, as the name suggests, refers to the mashing of cooked potatoes without using any butter, milk or cream.

CHAMP

1 onion, sliced
1½ cups milk (375 mL)
60 g butter
8 potatoes, cooked
4 shallots, finely diced
pepper, to taste

Cook onion in milk for 5 minutes. Add butter and potatoes to onion mixture and mash well. Add diced shallots and pepper. Serve with roasts, grills or fries.

Serves 6

POTATO DUMPLINGS

5 medium potatoes, cooked and mashed
½ teaspoon nutmeg
2 tablespoons semolina
3 tablespoons wholemeal flour
2 eggs, beaten
boiling water
1 chicken stock cube

Combine potatoes, nutmeg, semolina, wholemeal flour and eggs. With floured hands make mixture into balls. Boil water with stock cube and drop in dumplings. Simmer for 10 minutes. Serve with stews or soups.

Serves 6

TASTY VARIATIONS:
☐ Add 1 tablespoon chopped fresh chives or parsley and 1 tablespoon grated tasty cheese;
☐ add 1 rasher bacon, diced and fried;
☐ dumplings can be cooked in stew or soup the same way as in boiling water.

HASH BROWNS

4 medium potatoes, peeled
3 rashers bacon, rind removed and diced
butter or oil, for shallow-frying
1 onion, sliced
1 tablespoon chopped, fresh oregano

Parboil potatoes (or microwave on HIGH 5 minutes). Cut into medium-sized slices. Fry bacon until fat is transparent. Add butter and fry onion and potato with bacon, turning until browned. Sprinkle with oregano.

Serves 6

STUFFINGS
Stuffing should loosely fill chicken as it will expand slightly when cooked.

Potato Dumplings in Golden Nugget Soup

1. Melt butter and add peeled garlic.

2. Stir in hot milk and pepper.
3. Mash potatoes, then combine with sauce.

GARLIC MASHED POTATOES

2 heads of garlic, about 30 cloves
40 g butter
4 large potatoes, peeled
1 tablespoon flour
1 cup hot milk (250 mL)
pepper, to taste

Separate the garlic cloves and cook in boiling water for 2 minutes; cool and peel.

Melt butter in a heavy-based pan and add peeled garlic. Cover and cook on low heat for 15–20 minutes until tender but not browned. Meanwhile cook potatoes for 20 minutes or until tender (or microwave on HIGH for 6–8 minutes). Remove butter-garlic mixture from heat and stir in flour. Return to heat and cook 1 minute.

Remove from heat again and stir in hot milk and pepper. Bring to the boil and simmer until thickened, stirring all the time. (To microwave, combine garlic, butter and flour in a bowl and microwave on HIGH 1 minute. Stir in hot milk and pepper and microwave on HIGH 3 minutes until mixture boils. Remove from microwave and beat well.)

Push sauce through a seive or blend until smooth, return to heat and simmer 2 minutes (or microwave on MEDIUM 2 minutes). Drain and mash potatoes, and combine with sauce. Serve with any roast or poultry.

Serves 6

CALCANNON

This is a traditional Irish dish.

2 small cabbages, roughly chopped
2 leeks, diced
1 small onion, diced
4 medium potatoes, cooked and dry
**   mashed**
2 tablespoons cream
40 g butter
freshly ground black pepper

Boil cabbage, leeks and onion together in a small amount of water until they are tender; drain and mash.

Combine all ingredients and reheat stirring constantly (or microwave on HIGH 2 minutes). Serve with any meats, fish or poultry.

Serves 4

POTATO CASTLE

1 bunch spinach (or silver beet),
**   washed**
4 medium potatoes, peeled and
**   cooked**
40 g butter
milk, to mix
2 tablespoons pine nuts
1 clove garlic, crushed
6 hardboiled eggs, shelled

CHEESE SAUCE
40 g butter
1 tablespoon flour
1 cup milk (250 mL)
50 g grated tasty cheese

Boil or steam spinach until tender.

To make the Cheese Sauce, melt butter in a pan. Stir in flour and cook 1 minute. Remove from heat and stir in milk. Return to heat and cook until sauce thickens, stirring all the time (or microwave butter on HIGH 30 seconds, add flour and cook on HIGH 1 minute. Stir in milk and cook on HIGH 2 minutes, remove and beat well). Add cheese and stir until melted. Set aside to keep warm.

Mash potatoes with 20 g butter and enough milk to form a smooth paste. Drain spinach and cut finely. Melt 20 g butter and gently fry pine nuts and garlic for 1 minute. Add to spinach.

Place spoonfuls of spinach mixture on six entree plates. Top with a mound of potato. Cut eggs in half. On each plate, arrange two egg halves on top of the potato. Pour over Cheese Sauce and serve at once.

Serves 6

CARROT AND POTATO CASSEROLE

6 medium potatoes, peeled and sliced
1 onion, sliced
80 g butter
300 mL sour cream
1 teaspoon nutmeg
1 chicken stock cube
4 large carrots, peeled and sliced
1 tablespoon milk

Boil potatoes and onion until tender. Drain, reserving 2 tablespoons cooking liquid. Mash with 40 g butter, the sour cream and nutmeg. Crumble stock cube over carrots, just cover with water and boil carrots until tender. Drain and mash with reserved 2 tablespoons potato cooking liquid.

Spoon half the mashed potato into a greased casserole. Cover with all the mashed carrot, and top with remaining mashed potato. Brush with 1 tablespoon milk and dot with 40 g butter. Bake at 180°C (350°F) for approximately 20 minutes or until browned on top. Serve with steaks, roasts and poultry.

Serves 6.

BAKED CREAMED POTATOES

4 medium potatoes, cooked
1 cup mayonnaise (250 mL)
½ cup sour cream (125 mL)
3 tablespoons milk
2 eggs, beaten
2 teaspoons French mustard
3 tablespoons grated tasty cheese

Mash potatoes with mayonnaise, sour cream, milk, eggs and mustard.

Spoon into a greased ovenproof dish and top with cheese. Bake at 180°C (350°F) for 20–30 minutes (or microwave on HIGH 7 minutes or until the cheese bubbles). Serve with roasts and grills.

Serves 6

TASTY VARIATIONS:
☐ Replace mayonnaise with 1 cup sour cream (250 mL) and ½ cup milk (125 mL);
☐ sprinkle 4 rashers, diced and cooked bacon on top with the cheese.

HAM AND POTATO SCONES

4 medium potatoes, cooked and
**   mashed**
4 mushrooms, finely diced
4 slices ham, finely diced
1 onion, finely diced
3 tablespoons flour
20 g butter
1 egg, beaten
salt and pepper, to taste
oil, for shallow-frying

Combine all ingredients except oil. Turn onto a floured board and knead until smooth. Roll out like a large sausage. Cut into 10 slices.

Heat oil and fry each slice until browned on both sides. Serve with butter for morning tea.

Serves 6

TASTY VARIATIONS:

Replace ham with:
☐ 1 cup cooked and diced chicken (125 g);
☐ 4 rashers bacon, diced and lightly cooked;
☐ 2 tablespoons grated tasty cheeses.

Replace mushrooms with:
☐ 1 tomato, finely chopped;
☐ ½ capsicum, seeded and diced;
☐ 2 tablespoons corn kernels, drained.
Replace onion with:
☐ 2 shallots, diced;
☐ 1 tablespoon chopped fresh chives, or parsley.

Vegetarian Delights

With the increasing emphasis on health these days, more people are looking for alternatives to meat, chicken and fish. We have included plenty of tasty meatless recipes in this section and throughout the book, to satisfy both your nutritional needs and your taste buds.

POTATO CURRY

4 tablespoons oil
2 onions, sliced
1 clove garlic, crushed
4 potatoes, peeled and diced
½ teaspoon each: ground tumeric, cumin, cinnamon, cardamon, black pepper, ginger, and chilli powder
½ teaspoon sugar
1 tablespoon coconut milk
1 cup water (250 mL)
425 g canned tomatoes, liquid drained and reserved

ACCOMPANIMENTS
1 cup sour cream or natural (unflavoured) yoghurt (250 mL) mixed with 1 green cucumber, sliced
4 hardboiled eggs, crumbled
2 bananas peeled and sliced with a squeeze of lemon juice
4 tablespoons mango chutney
425 g pineapple pieces, drained
12 pappadums

Heat oil, add onion and fry until transparent (or microwave on HIGH 2 minutes). Add garlic and potatoes and fry 2 minutes more. Add remaining ingredients, bring to the boil and simmer 30 minutes or until potato is cooked.

Serve curry with rice, and accompaniments in separate bowls.

Serves 6

Handy hint: Leaving a metal spoon in a saucepan of simmering rice prevents water from boiling over.

TASTY VARIATIONS:
☐ With onions fry 2 eggplants, diced, salted and washed;
☐ 1 bunch spinach or silver beet, washed, shredded and cooked until tender. Add after 30 minutes of cooking;
☐ With onions fry 4 zucchini, diced and 2 shallots, diced;
☐ 500 g sliced butter beans (fresh or frozen) and 2 carrots, scraped and diced. Cook with potatoes.

OLD WIVES' TALES
Rub a raw potato on a wart, then bury the potato; as the potato rots so the wart will go.

Wrap grated potatoes on frostbite or burns.

Wrap a raw grated potato in a cloth and place over the eyes for 15 minutes; this is said to remove wrinkles.

Wrap a slice of baked potato in a stocking and tie around the throat to cure sore throats and rheumatism.

Write the name of an enemy on a piece of paper, stick it into a potato and the victim will die within the month.

Use the water from a boiled potato to cure a sprain.

Potato Curry served with traditional accompaniments — boiled rice, crispy pappadums, sliced banana, diced cucumber and yoghurt

POTATO FLAPJACKS

These make an ideal breakfast, served with eggs, bacon or grills.

1 egg
1 cup flour (125 g)
2 cups milk (500 mL)
6 medium potatoes, peeled and grated
3 tablespoons oil

Combine egg, flour and milk in a blender; process for 30 seconds. Add potatoes, 1 tablespoon at a time and blend until smooth. Heat a little oil in a pan and pour in 1 tablespoon of potato mixture (3 tablespoons for large flapjacks). Move the pan to spread mixture over base. Fry both sides until brown and crisp.

Serves 6

CHEESE AND POTATO FRITTERS

1 cup self-raising flour (125 g)
1 cup grated tasty cheese (125 g)
1 onion, grated
4 medium potatoes, peeled and grated
2 eggs, beaten
1 teaspoon nutmeg
½ cup evaporated milk (125 mL)
oil, for deep-frying
chutney, to serve

In a bowl combine all ingredients except for oil and chutney, and beat well to make a thick batter. Stand for 5 minutes. Heat oil and drop in batter, 1 tablespoon at a time. Cook both sides until golden. Serve with a teaspoon of chutney as an accompaniment to roasts, grills or fries.

Serves 6

TASTY VARIATIONS:
☐ Add 2 tablespoons canned corn kernels and 1 tablespoon capsicum diced;
☐ 1 carrot, scraped and grated, and 2 shallots, diced;
☐ ¼ teaspoon each ground chilli powder, cumin, turmeric and ½ tablespoon lemon juice.

POTATOES AND YOGHURT

An ideal accompaniment to grilled or roast lamb.

2 tablespoons oil
12 tiny new potatoes, washed and sliced
pinch ground cloves
½ teaspoon ground cinnamon
2 bay leaves
½ teaspoon crushed fresh ginger root
2 tablespoons chopped mixed fresh herbs
200 mL natural (unflavoured) yoghurt

Heat oil in frying pan. Add new potatoes, cloves, cinnamon, bay leaves and ginger root. Stir-fry for 2 minutes, then stir in herbs and yoghurt and heat through without boiling. Remove bay leaves and serve in an attractive serving bowl.

Serves 6

Note: Crush ginger root in a garlic crusher.

ARABIAN MIXED VEGETABLES

2 tablespoons oil or butter
1 onion, sliced
1 bay leaf
1 tablespoon chopped fresh dill
½ stalk celery, finely diced
1 potato, peeled and diced
1 carrot, scraped and diced
1 green-skinned apple, cored and diced
2 tomatoes, diced
2 small zucchini, diced
¼ cauliflower, divided into florets

Heat oil in pan, add onion and fry until transparent. Add all vegetables and herbs. Stir-fry for 2 minutes, lower heat and simmer for 10 minutes (or microwave, replacing oil with butter on HIGH 4 minutes).

To serve, remove bay leaf and place in a serving bowl.

Serves 6

TASTY VARIATIONS:
☐ Add 1 tablespoon sultanas;
☐ 1 tablespoon nuts.

VEGETARIAN PIE

1 cup red lentils (180 g)
½ cup chick peas (175 g)
2 cups water (500 mL)
2 vegetable stock cubes
1 tablespoon oil or butter
2 onions, sliced
1 clove garlic, crushed
125 g green beans, strung and sliced
1 red capsicum, seeded and diced
310 g canned tomato puree
1 tablespoon Worcestershire sauce
1 tablespoon tomato sauce
pinch dried oregano
pepper, to taste
3 medium potatoes, cooked and
    mashed
2 tablespoons chopped fresh parsley
2 tablespoons milk
40 g butter
paprika

Pour water over lentils and chick peas, cover and soak overnight. Drain well.

Cook chick peas in water with crumbled stock cubes for 30 minutes, then add lentils and cook a further 30 minutes or until tender. Drain and set aside.

Heat oil, add onions and gently fry until transparent. Add garlic, beans, capsicum and stir-fry for 2 minutes (or combine butter instead of oil, onions, garlic, beans and capsicum and microwave on HIGH 2 minutes).

Add tomato puree, both sauces and the seasonings. Bring to the boil and simmer for 2 minutes (or microwave on HIGH 2 minutes). Spoon lentils and peas into a greased casserole dish and pour over tomato mixture.

Combine mashed potatoes with parsley, milk and butter, and spread over tomato mixture. Sprinkle with a little paprika and bake at 180°C (350°F) for 20 minutes (or microwave on HIGH 4 minutes). Serve warm with salad and crusty bread.

Serves 6

TASTY VARIATION:
☐ Top with grated cheese and bake until brown (or microwave until cheese bubbles).

GNOCCHI WITH TASTY CHEESE SAUCE

3 medium potatoes, peeled and sliced
2 eggs, beaten
1½ cups flour (185 g)

TASTY CHEESE SAUCE
40 g butter
1 tablespoon flour
1 cup milk (250 mL)
1 cup grated tasty cheese (125 g)
1 teaspoon dry mustard

Boil potatoes until tender. Drain, reserving water in pan. Mash potatoes well with eggs. Add flour and mix to a dry dough. Turn out onto a floured board and knead well until smooth (about 2 minutes).

Divide mixture into four. Roll each piece into a sausage shape and cut into 2.5 cm slices. Press gently against a grater or a fork to 'roughen' the surface. Add 1 cup extra water to the reserved water in the pan and bring to the boil. Drop each gnocchi into the boiling water — they will drop to the bottom then rise. Boil for 1 minute after gnocchi rises to top of pan, then remove from pan with a slotted spoon. Drain on kitchen paper towels.

To make sauce, melt butter in a pan and stir in flour for 1 minute. Remove from heat and stir in milk to combine. Return to heat and stir until mixture boils and thickens. (Alternatively, microwave butter on HIGH 30 seconds then stir in flour, cook on HIGH 1 minute. Add milk, stir and cook on HIGH 2 minutes then beat well.)

Add cheese and mustard and stir until cheese melts. To serve, place cooked gnocchi in a greased casserole dish. Pour sauce over and brown under griller (or microwave on HIGH until cheese bubbles).

> STORAGE
> Store potatoes in a dark, cool spot in brown paper bags. New potatoes are best kept in the refrigerator, also in paper bags as the paper absorbs moisture.

Gnocchi with Tasty Cheese Sauce

BIRDS NEST

750 g broccoli or 8 fresh spinach (or silver beet) leaves
100 g butter
1 clove garlic, crushed
2 tablespoons flour
1 cup milk (250 mL)
6 eggs, separated
12 tiny new potatoes, washed (see Note)
3 tablespoons chopped fresh mint or parsley
Parmesan cheese, to serve

Soak broccoli or spinach in warm water (see *Note*) for 5 minutes. Shake well and boil for 10 minutes. Drain and mash broccoli or cut spinach very finely. Preheat oven to 180°C (375°F).

Melt 60 g butter in a pan, add garlic and gently fry but do not allow to brown. Stir in flour for 1 minute. Remove from heat and stir in milk. Return to heat and allow to boil and thicken, stirring all the time.

(Alternatively, microwave butter and garlic on HIGH 30 seconds, stir in flour and cook on HIGH 1 minute. Add milk and cook on HIGH 2 minutes, remove and beat well.)

Beat in egg yolks and add broccoli. Whisk egg whites until stiff and whisk into vegetable mixture. Spoon mixture into a greased 20 cm ring tin. Stand tin in a baking dish with 2.5 cm warm water and bake for 45 minutes.

Boil new potatoes until tender (or microwave potatoes, covered and with 1 teaspoon water, on HIGH 6 minutes).

Melt remaining 40 g butter in a pan (or microwave on HIGH 30 seconds). Add chopped mint and toss in new potatoes until coated. Place in a covered dish in oven to keep warm.

When souffle is cooked, place a large serving dish on top of the ring tin, carefully turn the plate over and gently turn out souffle.

Fill centre with new potatoes and sprinkle with Parmesan cheese. Serve with crusty bread and tomato.

Serves 6

Note: Warm water draws out any grit and insects in broccoli and spinach.

440 g canned potatoes are ideal for this recipe. Drain and wash in warm water, as there is no need to cook them.

1. Melt butter and garlic; stir in milk.

2. Beat in egg yolks and broccoli; add stiffened egg whites.

3. Spoon into a greased ring tin and stand tin in water.

4. When cooked, place a serving dish on top of ring tin and invert.

5. Fill centre with potatoes and sprinkle with Parmesan.

GOLDEN NUGGET SOUP

**6 small golden nugget pumpkins,
    washed
2 medium potatoes, peeled and sliced
1 onion, sliced
2 cups water (500 mL)
½ cup cream (125 mL)
croutons, to serve**

Slice the top off each pumpkin, scoop out the seeds and pour 1 tablespoon water into each pumpkin. Cook in an 180°C (350°F) oven until the insides are tender (or microwave on HIGH 15 minutes). Combine potatoes and onion in a pan, add water, bring to the boil and simmer for 30 minutes.

Cool pumpkins slightly, remove pulp and add to the potato soup. Heat shells in the oven at 180°C (350°F) for 10 minutes (or microwave on HIGH 2 minutes just before serving). Blend or push soup through a sieve. Reheat but do not boil (or microwave on HIGH 5 minutes).

To serve, spoon soup into pumpkin shells. Swirl in cream. Put pumpkins in a bowl if they need steadying, and serve with a bowl of croutons.

Serves 6

CARROT SOUP

**60 g butter
2 onions, sliced
2 large potatoes, peeled and sliced
2 stalks celery, diced
4 carrots, scraped and sliced
1 litre water
1 teaspoon sugar
1 clove garlic, crushed
pepper, to taste
½ cup cream (125 mL)**

Melt butter, add onions and fry until transparent. Add potatoes, celery, and carrots and fry for a further minute. Add water, sugar, garlic and pepper. Bring to the boil, lower heat and simmer for 30 minutes.

Blend or push through a sieve. Reheat (or microwave on HIGH 5 minutes). Serve in a tureen or soup bowls with a swirl of cream on top.

Serves 6

TASTY VARIATION:
☐ Replace carrots with 6 zucchinis, sliced or 1.5 kg pumpkin.

Tomato Cream Soup

POTATO PEEL STOCK

This recipe can be used to replace water in all the soup recipes in this book. Prepare it when next peeling potatoes.

**washed potato peels of 6 potatoes
1 onion, sliced
2 carrots, scraped and sliced
1 stalk celery, diced
1.25 litres water**

Combine all ingredients in a pan and bring to the boil. Lower heat and simmer for 1½ hours. As the water evaporates, add a little more to keep the vegetables covered.

Strain and discard vegetables. Store stock in refrigerator or freeze until required.

Makes 1 L

TASTY VARIATION:
☐ Serve the stock as soup. Discard potato peels only and serve.

TOMATO CREAM SOUP

**2 leeks
40 g butter
500 g tomatoes, peeled and roughly
    chopped
3 large potatoes, peeled and sliced
1 teaspoon sugar
2½ cups water (625 mL)
½ cup sour cream (125 mL)
chopped fresh parsley and croutons,
    to serve**

Finely slice only the white part of the leek. Melt butter, add leek and gently fry for 1 minute. Remove from heat and add chopped tomatoes. Return to heat, stirring until tomatoes soften. Add potatoes, sugar and water and bring to the boil. Lower heat and simmer for 30 minutes.

Blend until smooth. Stir in cream and carefully reheat (or pour into a bowl and microwave on MEDIUM until soup steams). Do not allow soup to boil as the cream will curdle. Serve with a sprinkle of parsley and a few croutons.

Serves 4

POTATO AND AVOCADO SOUP

3 cups water (750 mL)
2 vegetable stock cubes
2 large potatoes, peeled and sliced
3 onions, sliced
2 ripe avocados, peeled and sliced
2 teaspoons lemon juice
300 mL cream
2 teaspoons nutmeg

Combine water, crumbled stock cubes, potatoes and onions in a pan and bring to the boil. Lower heat and simmer for 30 minutes. Blend until smooth.

Blend or puree avocados with lemon juice and ½ cup of potato liquid.

Heat both soups in separate pans (or microwave on HIGH 4 minutes). Stir cream into the avocado soup. Pour the soups into separate jugs. Holding a jug in each hand, pour soups into individual bowls at the same time, then gently swirl with a knife. Sprinkle with nutmeg.

Serves 6

TASTY VARIATION:
☐ Replace avocado soup with 2½ cups (625 mL) Carrot Soup (see recipe).

POTATO SAMBAL

4 medium potatoes, peeled and diced
2 green chillies, diced
½ teaspoon chilli powder
½ onion, finely diced
1 teaspoon olive oil
½ lemon juice
Poori (see recipe), to serve

Boil potatoes until tender (or microwave with 1 teaspoon water on HIGH 8 minutes). Combine with all remaining ingredients and serve with Poori (see recipe).

Serves 6 as a side dish

POORI

500 g plain or wholemeal flour
cold water
extra flour
120 g ghee or unsalted butter

Sift flour, add sufficient cold water to make a stiff dough. Cover with a damp cloth and leave for 1 hour. Knead with a little extra flour until smooth and shape into small balls. Heat ghee in a pan and put in one ball at a time, pressing balls flat with a spatula. Cook both sides until balls puff up. Drain on kitchen paper towel and serve at once.

Serves 6

DAHIN ALOO

Dahin is Indian for yoghurt and Aloo means potatoes. For a truly exotic touch, serve this Indian speciality with pappadums.

60 g ghee or unsalted butter
1 onion, sliced
1 teaspoon peeled and finely sliced fresh ginger root
1 red chilli, finely chopped
1 tablespoon ground coriander
1 teaspoon ground tumeric
pinch mace
2 tomatoes, peeled and chopped
200 mL natural (unflavoured) yoghurt
1 teaspoon sugar
4 tablespoons raisins
6 potatoes, peeled, cooked and sliced
pappadums, to serve

Heat ghee in a pan. Add onion and ginger and fry until onion is transparent. Add chilli, spices, tomatoes, yoghurt and sugar. Simmer until thick. Add raisins and potatoes and heat through. Serve with pappadums.

Serves 6

DOSA WITH POTATO STUFFING

180 g rice flour
180 g flour
½ teaspoon chilli powder or more, to taste
2 tablespoons natural (unflavoured) yoghurt
20 g ghee
water, to mix
oil, for shallow-frying

STUFFING
20 g ghee
1 onion, finely diced
¼ teaspoon mustard seeds
¼ teaspoon ground turmeric
¼ teaspoon chilli powder
2 potatoes peeled, diced and cooked

Combine flours, chilli powder, yoghurt, ghee and sufficient water to make a thick batter. Cover with damp cloth and stand overnight at room temperature.

Next day, heat oil and pour 1 tablespoon batter at a time. Fry both sides until golden. Repeat until all the mixture is used. Set aside and keep warm.

To make stuffing, heat ghee in pan and fry onion until transparent. Add all seasonings and potatoes and heat through. Spoon a little mixture into the centre of each dosa and fold. Serve with roast meat or chicken curry.

Serves 6

TASTY VARIATIONS:
☐ Replace onion with 2 green chillies and seasonings with garam masala;
☐ add 250 g fresh green peas, cooked and 2 shallots, diced.

EGGPLANT AND POTATO BAKE

2 eggplants
salt
4 medium potatoes, peeled and sliced
1 tablespoon oil or butter
2 onions, sliced
1 cup grated cheese (125 g)

Slice eggplants and sprinkle with salt. Stand 30 minutes then rinse under cold water. Cook potatoes until tender (or microwave with 2 teaspoons water on HIGH 8 minutes, stand 3 minutes). Drain on kitchen paper towels.

Heat oil, add onions and fry until transparent (or microwave onions using butter in place of oil, on HIGH 2 minutes). Grease a casserole dish and arrange eggplant slices on base. Sprinkle lightly with cheese, cover with a layer of potato, top with onion and a little more cheese. Repeat until all vegetables are used, finishing with cheese.

Cover dish and bake at 180°F (350°F) for 1¼ hours. Remove lid and bake a further 15 minutes. Serve as a main meal or as a side dish with grilled meat.

Serves 6

TASTY VARIATIONS:
Add any of the following:
☐ 2 tomatoes, sliced;
☐ 2 carrots, scraped and sliced;
☐ 2 zucchini, sliced;
☐ combine 2 eggs, ½ cup milk (125 mL), pinch nutmeg, pour over vegetables, then top with remaining cheese and bake;
☐ top with 1.5 kg mashed pumpkin combined with 1 egg white, whisked then sprinkle with remaining cheese, and bake.

> EGGPLANTS
> Sprinkling salt on sliced eggplant takes away the bitter juices: Don't forget to rinse the eggplants and drain before using.

Fabulous Fries

Diets notwithstanding, most of us love the occasional excursion into fried foods, and they are often family favourites. Chips, scallops, croquettes, crispy potatoes, pommes noisettes - homemade is infinitely superior to prepackaged foods. Eaten in moderation, i.e. once a week, they shouldn't damage your health or your waistline.

PERUVIAN BALLS IN SPICY PEANUT SAUCE

40 g butter
2 onions, sliced
4 large potatoes, cooked and
  dry mashed
250 g Munster cheese, grated
oil, for shallow-frying

SPICY PEANUT SAUCE
5 tablespoons oil or butter
1 onion, grated
150 g raw, shelled peanuts
  or 1 cup peanut butter (250 g)
2 chillies, finely diced
3 cloves garlic, crushed
½ cup warm water (125 mL)
1 tablespoon brown sugar
1 tablespoon soy sauce
2 tablespoons lemon juice

Melt butter, add onions and gently fry until transparent (or microwave butter and onions on HIGH 2 minutes). Combine with potatoes and cheese. Divide into 12 balls, flattening each slightly with the back of a tablespoon. Chill until ready to use.

To make sauce, heat oil, add onion and fry until transparent (or substitute butter for oil and microwave on HIGH 2 minutes). In a blender combine with all remaining sauce ingredients and process until smooth. Pour puree into a pan, bring to the boil and simmer for 3 minutes to thicken.

Heat oil in a frying pan and fry flattened balls on both sides until golden. Serve with Spicy Peanut Sauce. This dish goes well with roast chicken and green salad.

Serves 6

PARATHAS

2 cups flour (250 g)
2 cups wholemeal flour (270 g)
40 g butter
1 cup warm water (250 mL)
oil, for shallow-frying

FILLING
2 medium potatoes, cooked and
  dry mashed
125 g grated tasty cheese
2 teaspoons Chinese five-spice

Sift flours together in a bowl. Rub in butter with fingertips. Stir in water with a knife and mix to a firm dough. Turn out onto a floured board and knead until smooth. Cover and let stand for 10 minutes.

Divide dough into six portions. Roll each section into a circle approximately 1 cm in diameter.

Combine filling ingredients. Place a spoonful of filling in the centre of each circle and roll into a ball. Flatten with a rolling pin into 10 cm circles.

Heat oil in a frying pan and fry flattened balls on both sides until golden. Serve with Spicy Peanut Sauce. This dish goes well with roast chicken and green salad.

Serves 6

BURGHUL AND POTATO BALLS

1 cup burghul (140 g)
6 medium potatoes, cooked and
  dry mashed
1 cup flour (125 g)
pepper, to taste

FILLING
2 onions, sliced
2 tablespoons water
¼ teaspoon ground allspice
¼ cup pine nuts (40 g)
¼ cup currants (40 g)
2 tablespoons tahina
oil, for deep frying

Place burghul in a bowl and cover with water. Soak for 5 minutes, then drain, pressing burghul with a spoon to remove water. Combine mashed potatoes, burghul, flour and pepper.

To make the filling, place onions in a pan with the water. Boil for 10 minutes then drain (or microwave onions with 2 teaspoons water on HIGH 4 minutes). Add all filling ingredients to onions, stirring well to combine.

Take one tablespoon of mixture and roll into a ball by hand. Flatten out, place a spoonful of filling in the centre, then reshape into a ball. Repeat until both mixtures are used. Heat oil and fry balls until golden. Serve as nibbles with drinks.

Serves 6

Note: Burghul is hulled wheat and is available at supermarkets, delicatessens and health food stores. It is also known as "bulkar (Arabic)", "pourgouri" (Greek) and "bular" (Turkish). Tahina is a paste made from crushed sesame seeds. It can also be bought from delicatessens and some health food stores.

FRYING
There are 3 types of frying:
☐ shallow-frying which is ideal for leftovers and uses approximately 2.5 cm of heated oil in a pan;
☐ pan-frying, a delicious way of cooking leftovers or thinly sliced potatoes in approximately 1 tablespoon of heated oil in a pan;
☐ deep-frying, which is either for cooking or reheating and uses hot oil in a deep-fryer.

Peruvian Balls in Spicy Peanut Sauce

PERFECT CHIPS

The potato chip was originally known as the 'Saratoga Chip'. It was invented by an Indian cook with the unlikely name of George Crumb, in Saratoga. He finely sliced the potato and then quickly fried it in hot fat.

6 medium old potatoes, peeled and washed
oil, for deep-frying
salt (optional)

Slice potatoes lengthways into fine strips. Place in a bowl of iced water for 10 minutes minimum, preferably 1–2 hours. Drain and dry well on absorbent paper.

Heat the oil to 190°C (375°F). Place chips in a frying basket and lower carefully into the hot oil. Fry for 5–8 minutes, then remove and drain. At this point, the chips are 'blanched' and can stand for several hours until ready for the final cooking. (Once blanched they can be refrigerated, covered, for up to 4 hours, then fried and served.)

Increase oil temperature to 200°C (400°F) and cook chips for the second time until they are crisp and golden (about 3–5 minutes). Drain on absorbent kitchen paper and serve at once.

Serves 4

1. Soak uncooked chips in iced water for 10 minutes minimum.

FRENCH FRIES OR CHIPS?
French fries were created in France by Antonine Parmentier, who served them at a dinner in honour of Benjamin Franklin. Franklin cannot have been too impressed, as it was left to Thomas Jefferson to introduce French fries to America at a White House dinner.

What is the difference?
French fries differ from chips in both size and method of cooking. French fries are sliced into very thin strips and deep-fried in oil.

Chips were originally cut into thicker strips and deep-fried in animal fat (suet). Nowadays, fries and chips are generally both fried in oil but may still retain their difference in size.

2. Blanch chips 5–8 minutes.

3. Drain well on absorbent kitchen paper.

WHICH OIL?

Oil is a refined liquid made from extracts of seeds, nuts, fruits and occasionally animal fats. Cooking oils have been processed to be relatively flavourless, odourless and to keep for a period of time. They are divided into five groups:

Delicate, aromatic oils (e.g. sesame, walnut, grape)
These oils should be always stored in the refrigerator. Use sparingly in salads and for stir-frying.

Polyunsaturated oils (e.g. sunflower, safflower, maize and some blended oils)
Believed to help control blood fats, these oils can be used in deep- or shallow-frying, as they have a good tolerance to high temperatures.

Mono unsaturated (e.g. peanut, olive and sesame)
These oils break down at high temperatures and should not be used for deep-frying. They have an excellent flavour for salads. If the flavour is too strong, reduce by mixing an equal quantity of polyunsaturated oil (olive oil, particularly virgin olive oil, is excellent for salads).

Saturated oils (e.g. coconut and animal oils)
These oils are very strong and not really recommended for general cooking.

Solidified oils
These are processed to make them solid at room temperature. They are slightly cheaper and are recommended for deep- and shallow-frying. Available from supermarkets. Used and unused oils should never be mixed. Buy only sufficient oil to be used within two months. Oils may be used several times, strained and stored (except for aromatic oils) in a tightly sealed container away from light.

CAUTION: If you overheat your oil and it begins to 'smoke', this is a sign that the oil has started to break down and should be discarded. The smokey taste will penetrate the food, and at this stage the oil can easily burst into flames.

4. Fry for the second time until golden, 3–5 minutes.

BAKED SALMON CROQUETTES WITH QUICK TOMATO SAUCE

440 g canned salmon, drained
1 onion, diced
2 eggs, beaten
2 tablespoons mayonnaise
1 tablespoon chopped fresh parsley
2 medium potatoes, cooked and dry mashed
1 tablespoon water
1½–2 cups dried breadcrumbs (185 g–250 g)
1 tablespoon grated Parmesan cheese

TOMATO SAUCE
4 tablespoons tomato sauce
1 onion, diced
½ chicken stock cube
1 tablespoon water

Remove bones from salmon and crumble fish into a bowl. Combine with onion, 1 egg, mayonnaise, parsley and mashed potatoes. Take spoonfuls and mould into croquette shapes (oval). Refrigerate for 1 hour.

Mix the other egg with water and, in another bowl mix breadcrumbs with cheese. Dip croquettes into egg-mixture then toss in breadcrumb-cheese mixture. Refrigerate a further 1 hour.

Arrange croquettes in a greased baking dish and bake at 180°C (350°F) for 15–20 minutes.

Mix sauce ingredients together in a pan and bring to the boil (or microwave on HIGH 2 minutes). Remove from heat, stir well and pour into a sauce boat.

Serves 6

TASTY VARIATIONS:
☐ For a delicious meal serve with chips and a green salad;
☐ add a dash of Worcestershire or Tabasco sauce to tingle the taste buds.

CHEESE CROQUETTES WITH MUSTARD SAUCE

2 medium potatoes, cooked
40 g butter
1 egg yolk
2 tablespoons milk
80 g grated tasty cheese
2 tablespoons chopped fresh parsley
1 egg, beaten
2 tablespoons water
1½–2 cups dried breadcrumbs (185 g–250 g)
2 tablespoons almond halves
oil, for deep-frying

SAUCE
40 g butter
1 tablespoon flour
¼ cup water (60 mL)
¼ cup cream (60 mL)
2 teaspoons French mustard

Mash potatoes with butter, egg yolk, milk, cheese and parsley. Take tablespoonfuls of mixture and form into croquette shapes (oval); chill for 1 hour. Mix egg and water together. Dip croquettes in egg-water mixture, then breadcrumbs, then press in almond halves. Chill for a further 1 hour.

To make sauce, melt butter and stir in flour. Cook 1 minute, then remove from heat and stir in water, cream, and mustard. Return to heat and stir until sauce boils and thickens.

(Alternatively, microwave butter on HIGH 1 minute, add flour and cook on HIGH 1 minute. Stir in water, cream and mustard and cook on MEDIUM 2 minutes. Remove and stir well.)

Heat oil and deep-fry croquettes until golden. Drain on kitchen paper towels. To serve, arrange croquettes on plates, pour sauce over and serve with grills, roasts or fish.

Serves 6

SMOKED FISH CAKES WITH TARTARE SAUCE

250 g potatoes, mashed
250 g canned smoked fish, flaked
salt and pepper, to taste
pinch nutmeg ground
1 tablespoon finely chopped fresh parsley
1 tablespoon lemon juice
1 egg, beaten
dried breadcrumbs, to coat

TARTARE SAUCE
1 cup mayonnaise (250 mL)
2 tablespoons gherkins
1 tablespoon capers
finely chopped fresh parsley, to taste

Combine mashed potatoes with all remaining fish cake ingredients. Shape into small balls, dip in beaten egg and coat with breadcrumbs.

Heat oil in a pan until hot — 190°C (375°F). Fry cakes until golden on both sides. Drain on absorbent kitchen paper and serve with sauce.

To make sauce, combine all sauce ingredients in a bowl and mix together to a smooth consistency. Store in a well-sealed glass jar. Will keep refrigerated for up to ten days.

Serves 4

POMMES DE TERRE BERNY

4 large potatoes, cooked and dry mashed
2 eggs
2 tablespoons cream
2 tablespoons self-raising flour
2 tablespoons flour
2 tablespoons water
1½ cups flaked almonds (180 g)
oil, for deep-frying

Combine mashed potatoes with 1 egg, cream, and self-raising flour. Mix well. If mixture is too soft, add extra flour. Place flour in a plastic bag. Drop in spoonfuls of potato mixture and toss until lightly covered with flour. Remove and roll into balls.

Mix the other egg and water. Dip potato balls in egg-water mixture then roll in flaked almonds. Chill until ready to use. Heat oil and fry balls until golden (the almonds will brown quickly). Serve with roasts, grilled meats or fish.

Serves 6

TASTY VARIATIONS:
Add to the potato mixture any of the following:
☐ 1 clove garlic, crushed;
☐ 1 tablespoon grated Parmesan cheese;
☐ 1 tablespoon chopped fresh parsley;
☐ 1 small onion, finely diced;
☐ replace cream with 2 tablespoons sour cream; replace almonds with 2 cups dried breadcrumbs (250 g).

CRISPY POTATOES

4 large potatoes, peeled, washed and diced
½ cup oil (125 mL), for shallow-frying

Pat potatoes dry with kitchen paper towel. Heat oil in a pan and add potatoes, stirring until tender.

Serves 6

CORN AND POTATO PUFFS

310 g canned corn kernels, drained
1 egg, beaten
2 tablespoons flour
4 medium potatoes, cooked and dry mashed
2 tablespoons chutney
2 tablespoons natural (unflavoured) yoghurt
1 red capsicum, seeded and finely diced
4 shallots, finely diced
2 cloves garlic, crushed
oil, for deep-frying

In a bowl, combine drained corn with beaten egg, flour, mashed potatoes, chutney, yoghurt, capsicum, shallots and garlic. Heat oil in a pan and fry spoonfuls of mixture until golden. Drain on kitchen paper towels and serve with roasts or grills or for breakfast, with eggs and bacon.

TASTY VARIATIONS:
Add to the mixture any of the following:
☐ 1 tablespoon grated Parmesan cheese;
☐ 1 tablespoon peas, cooked, or carrots, diced and cooked;
☐ 1 tablespoon bacon, diced and cooked.

POMMES NOISETTES

4 medium potatoes, peeled and washed
½ teaspoon salt
cold water
60 g butter

With a melon baller, scoop potato into balls. Place in salted cold water (make sure the potato balls are covered with water to prevent browning). Cover with a lid and stand for 1 hour, then drain.

Boil a large pan of water and cook potatoes 15 minutes (or microwave on HIGH approximately 5 minutes until tender). Drain and pat dry with kitchen paper towel. Melt butter in a pan and allow to foam. Add potatoes and stir until golden brown.

Serves 6

POTATO SCALLOPS

4 large potatoes, peeled and thinly sliced
flour, to dust
oil, for deep-frying

BATTER 1
1 tablespoon flour
1 cup self-raising flour (125 g)
water

BATTER 2
1 cup self-raising flour (125 g)
185 mL beer
flour, to dust

Dust potato slices with flour and heat oil in a deep-frier.

To make batter 1 place flours in a bowl and whisk in sufficient water to make a smooth batter. If you choose to make batter 2, place self-raising flour in a bowl and whisk in enough beer for a smooth batter.

Dip potato slices into batter of your choice — and if using batter 2, dust slices with flour — and fry in hot oil until lightly brown. Drain on kitchen paper towels. Just before serving, reheat oil and refry until golden; drain.

Serves 6

MOCK WHITEBAIT

2 large potatoes, peeled, washed and grated
1 tablespoon self-raising flour (see Note)
1 egg, beaten
water, to mix
oil, for shallow-frying
cooked bacon strips
tomato sauce, to serve

Place grated potatoes in a bowl. Add flour, egg and sufficient water to bind together. Heat oil and drop tablespoonfuls of mixture into pan. Flatten with the back of an egg slice. Cook both sides until golden and drain on kitchen paper towels.

To serve, accompany with strips of bacon or a little tomato sauce.

Serves 6

Note: If preparing this recipe ahead of time, use plain flour.

TASTY VARIATIONS:
☐ Add 1 small onion, grated, to the mixture before cooking;
☐ 1 tablespoon chopped fresh parsley or chives before cooking.

Pommes Noisettes and Corn and Potato Puffs

Fillings, Toppings and Stuffings

The versatile potato can form the basis for poultry stuffings, be used to make luscious fillings for potato cups, or be served with a variety of quick, easy toppings.

HERB STUFFING FOR CHICKEN

2 medium potatoes, cooked and dry mashed
3 onions, sliced
40 g butter
1 tablespoon fresh sage
pepper, to taste
1 egg
1 tablespoon chopped fresh thyme

Combine all ingredients and use to stuff a 1.5 kg chicken.

TASTY VARIATIONS:
Add or substitute any of the following:
☐ 4 fried mushrooms;
☐ 2 tablespoons corn kernels;
☐ 2 rashers bacon, diced and cooked;
☐ 2 stalks celery, diced.

ONION STUFFING

80 g butter
2 onions, diced
250 g sausage meat
1 large potato, cooked and dry mashed
1 egg
pepper, to taste
2 tablespoons chopped fresh parsley

Heat butter in a pan. Add onions and gently fry until transparent (or combine butter and onion in a dish, microwave on HIGH 2 minutes). Remove onion with a slotted spoon and mix thoroughly in a bowl with sausage meat, cooked potato, egg, pepper and parsley. Use for stuffing a 2 kg chicken or other poultry.

ROAST CHICKEN

1.5 kg chicken
2 tablespoons oil or butter

Pre-heat oven to 190°C (375°F). Season cavity of chicken with the stuffing of your choice. Place chicken in a oven pan with oil and roast for 1½–2 hours, basting frequently. If chicken sticks to the bottom of the pan, add more oil or butter.

Serves 4

FRUITY STUFFING

60 g butter
1 large onion, finely chopped
12 dried apricots, chopped
6 prunes, pitted and chopped
¼ cup sultanas (45 g)
¼ cup currants (40 g)
1 large apple, diced
½ teaspoon salt
¼ teaspoon pepper
¼ teaspoon ground cinnamon
1 teaspoon dried tarragon
½ teaspoon dried thyme
1½ teaspoons saffron threads
2 medium potatoes, cooked and dry mashed

Melt butter in a pan and fry chopped onion until tender but not brown. Add all remaining ingredients and cook a further 3 minutes. Remove from heat and use to stuff a 1.5 kg chicken.

A family favourite — roast chicken cooked with stuffing and a variety of vegetables

Fillings

Most fillings can be prepared a couple of hours before serving. To reheat, arrange filled potatoes on a tray and bake at 180°C (350°F) for 15 minutes (or microwave on HIGH 1 minute per potato).

MUSHROOM FILLING

6 Potato Cups (see recipe)
40 g butter
125 g mushrooms, sliced
grated tasty cheese

Prepare potato cups, reserving mashed potato pulp. Melt butter, add mushrooms and gently fry until tender (or microwave on HIGH 2 minutes). Combine mushrooms and potato and fill shells.

Top each shell with cheese. Reheat and brown cheese topping.

Fills 6 potatoes

CHICKEN AND ALMOND FILLING

6 Potato Cups (see recipe)
20 g butter
2 tablespoons almond halves
250 g cooked chicken, diced
2 tablespoons mayonnaise

Prepare potato cups, reserving mashed potato pulp. Melt butter, add almonds and fry until lightly browned. Combine with remaining ingredients. Spoon into shells and reheat.

Fills 6 potatoes

MEXICAN FILLING

6 Potato Cups (see recipe)
3 tablespoons canned baked beans
pinch chilli powder
2 tablespoons sour cream
grated tasty cheese
12 corn chips

Prepare potato cups, reserving mashed potato pulp. Combine baked beans, chilli powder, sour cream and mashed potato. Spoon into shells and top with cheese. Reheat and brown cheese topping. Serve with two cornchips poked into the top of each filled potato.

Fills 6 potatoes

Potato Cups

PRAWN FILLING

6 Potato Cups (see recipe)
40 g butter, melted
250 g cooked prawns, shelled,
**   deveined and halved**
1 teaspoon lemon juice
pepper, to taste
1 tablespoon chopped fresh chives

Prepare potato cups, reserving mashed potato pulp. Combine all ingredients. Spoon into shells and reheat.
Fills 6 potatoes

VEGETARIAN FILLING

6 Potato Cups (see recipe)
½ cup any green vegetables, cooked
**   and chopped**
1 tomato, chopped
1 tablespoon mayonnaise

Prepare potato cups, reserving mashed potato pulp. Combine all ingredients. Spoon into shells and reheat.

Fills 6 potatoes

SOUR CREAM AND SHALLOT FILLING

6 Potato Cups (see recipe)
20 g butter
2 shallots, diced
pepper, to taste
½ cup sour cream (125 mL)

Prepare 6 potato cups, reserving mashed potato pulp. Melt butter and fry shallots until tender (or microwave on HIGH 2 minutes). Add pepper, sour cream and mashed potato and mix well. Spoon mixture into the shells and reheat.

Fills 6 potatoes

BACON AND MUSHROOM FILLING

6 Potato Cups (see recipe)
4 rashers bacon, diced
40 g butter
125 g mushrooms, sliced

Prepare potato cups, reserving mashed potato pulp. Fry bacon in butter until crisp (or microwave butter and bacon on HIGH 2–3 minutes). Combine bacon and mashed potato. Gently fry mushrooms until tender (or microwave on HIGH 2 minutes). Fold into potato mixture, spoon into shells and reheat.

Fills 6 potatoes

73

AMERICAN FILLING

6 Potato Cups (see recipe)
2 tablespoons diced ham
1 tablespoon chopped fresh chives
2 teaspoons American mustard
3 tablespoons grated tasty cheese

Prepare potato cups, reserving mashed potato pulp. Combine all ingredients except cheese. Spoon into shells. Top with cheese. Reheat and brown cheese.

Fills 6 potatoes

TASTY VARIATION:
☐ Replace American mustard with 2 teaspoons French mustard.

CELERIAC FILLING

6 Potato Cups (see recipe)
20 g butter
1 celeriac root, peeled and diced
pepper, to taste
2 egg yolks, beaten
1 egg white, lightly whisked
6 slices Cheddar cheese

Prepare potato cups, reserving mashed potato pulp.

Melt butter, add celeriac and gently cook until tender (or microwave on HIGH 2 minutes). Combine celeriac, mashed potato, pepper, egg yolks and fold in egg white.

Spoon into shells. Top each potato shell with a slice of cheese, reheat and brown cheese.

Fills 6 potatoes

BLUE POTATO FILLING

6 Potato Cups (see recipe)
40 g butter
125 g blue vein cheese, mashed
1 tablespoon cream
1 tablespoon tomato sauce
½ teaspoon chopped fresh basil

Prepare potato cups, reserving mashed potato pulp. Melt butter in a pan (or microwave on HIGH 30 seconds). Add remaining ingredients and beat well. Spoon into shells and reheat.

Fills 6 potatoes

SEAFOOD FILLING

6 Potato Cups (see recipe)
105 g fish, cooked and flaked (see Note)
½ cup mayonnaise (125 mL)
2 tablespoons chopped fresh parsley

Prepare potato cups, reserving mashed potato pulp. Combine all filling ingredients. Spoon into shells and reheat.

Fills 6 potatoes

Note: Any fish is suitable; smoked haddock or cod are particularly delicious.

CHEESE AND CHUTNEY FILLING

6 Potato Cups (see recipe)
40 g butter
80 g grated tasty cheese
1 tablespoon chutney
1 celery stalk, finely diced

Prepare potato cups, reserving mashed potato pulp. Melt butter, add all filling ingredients and mix well. Spoon into shells and reheat.

Fills 6 potatoes

CURRIED EGG FILLING

6 Potato Cups (see recipe)
3 eggs, hardboiled, peeled and chopped
4 tablespoons mayonnaise
1 teaspoon curry powder
1 teaspoon garam masala

Prepare potato cups, reserving mashed potato pulp. Combine all ingredients. Spoon into shells and reheat.

Fills 6 potatoes

CRUNCHY CHEESE AND APPLE FILLING

6 Potato Cups (see recipe)
80 g blue vein cheese, mashed or crumbled
1 green apple, cored and diced (leave peel on)
2 tablespoons mayonnaise

Prepare potato cups, reserving mashed potato pulp. Combine all ingredients. Spoon into shells and reheat.

Fills 6 potatoes

SAVOURY BEEF AND BEAN FILLING

The mashed potato from Potato Cups recipe is not used in this Filling.

6 Potato Cups (see recipe)
1 tablespoon oil
1 onion, diced
500 g minced beef
2 tablespoons tomato sauce
2 tablespoons Worcestershire sauce
2 stalks celery, diced
2 tablespoons canned kidney beans washed and drained (optional)
1 tablespoon chopped fresh parsley

Prepare potato cups; set mashed potato pulp aside for use in another recipe.

Heat oil in a pan, add onion and fry until tender. Add mince, sauces, celery and kidney beans and cook for 15 minutes (or microwave on HIGH stirring occasionally for 8 minutes or until cooked).

Drain off excess liquid. Add parsley. Spoon into shells and reheat.

Fills 6 potatoes

TOMATO AND PRAWN FILLING

250 g cooked prawns
juice ½ lemon
20 g butter
1 tablespoon oil
1 onion, diced
1 tablespoon flour
4 tomatoes, chopped
1 tablespoon tomato paste
1 chicken stock cube
½ cup water (125 mL)

Place prawns in a bowl, squeeze over lemon juice and store in refrigerator until ready to use. If prawns are large, slice in half lengthways before marinating.

Melt butter and oil, add onion and fry until transparent. Stir in flour and cook 1 minute. (Alternatively, microwave butter, oil and onion on HIGH 2 minutes. Stir in flour and cook on HIGH 1 minute.)

Add tomatoes, tomato paste, stock cube and water and stir until sauce thickens. Simmer 5 minutes. (Alternatively, combine remaining ingredients, stir well and microwave on HIGH 5 minutes.)

Add prawns and lemon juice and stir until heated through.

Serves 6

TASTY VARIATION:
☐ Replace prawns and lemon juice with 4 rashers bacon, diced and fried with onion.

Tasty Toppings

All our toppings are quick and easy to prepare. No one could accuse the potato of being boring when served with one or more of the following:

- sour cream
- cottage cheese
- fresh herbs
- melted cheese
- diced crispy bacon or ham
- finely diced chilli

- toasted sesame seeds
- finely diced fried onion
- fried onion and tomato
- fried mushrooms
- fried mushrooms and onion

1. Rub potato with oil and wrap in foil.

2. Cut a criss-cross pattern in the top of each potato.

3. Spoon sour cream over potatoes.

Baking Day

Potatoes appear in bread recipes in many countries around the world. Originally used in times of grain shortages, potato bread is both economical and nutritious. It also makes particularly good toast and croutons. Cakes, biscuits and sweet rolls also come up light and fluffy, and make a delicious change from more conventional recipes.

IRISH SODA BREAD

2 cups flour (250 g)
1 cup self-raising flour (125 g)
1 teaspoon bicarbonate of soda
pinch salt
½ teaspoon sugar
20 g butter
2 potatoes, cooked and mashed
1¼ cups warmed buttermilk (300 mL)
1 egg, beaten

Sift flours together in a bowl. Add bicarbonate of soda, salt and sugar; mix well. Rub butter into flour until mixture resembles fine breadcrumbs. Mix in mashed potato.

Make a well in the centre and pour in combined buttermilk and beaten egg. Mix to a dough, form into a round loaf and place on a greased oven tray. Using a knife, mark bread into eight pieces, dust the top with a little flour and bake at 180°C (350°F) for 30–40 minutes. Cool before serving. To make a soft crust, brush with melted butter while hot.

Makes 1 loaf

POTATO GALETTE

40 g butter
1 onion, sliced
4 medium potatoes, cooked and
    mashed
1 egg, beaten
1 cup grated tasty cheese (125 g)
½ teaspoon dry mustard

Melt butter, add onion and gently fry until transparent (or microwave on HIGH 2 minutes). Combine with mashed potato, egg, cheese and mustard. Spoon mixture into a greased cake tin. Bake at 180°C (350°F) for 45 minutes. Turn out and cut into wedges. Serve as an accompaniment to roasts.

Serves 6

POTATO YEAST BREAD

15 g fresh yeast
1¼ tablespoons sugar
2 tablespoons warm water
3 potatoes, cooked and mashed
1 cup and 2 tablespoons warm milk
    (290 mL)
40 g butter
4 cups flour (500 g)
pinch salt
1 tablespoon fresh chopped chives

Crumble yeast into a small bowl. Add 1 teaspoon sugar and the warm water. Stir with a fork until yeast dissolves. In a large mixing bowl, combine yeast mixture, 2 tablespoons warm milk and the mashed potatoes. Set aside in a draught-free, warm place for 20 minutes.

Boil remaining milk (or microwave on HIGH 2 minutes). Add butter and stir until melted. Allow to cool slightly. Combine remaining tablespoon sugar, the flour, salt, chives and mashed potato to the bowl. Mix in. Make a well in the centre and add butter-milk mixture. Mix until combined. Turn dough out onto a floured board and knead well for 10 minutes until smooth and elastic.

Return dough to bowl, cover with a warm, damp cloth and stand in a warm place until dough has doubled in size (1½–2 hours). Turn out onto a floured board and 'punch' dough in centre, knead a further 10 minutes and place in a greased loaf tin. Cover with a warm damp cloth and leave in a warm place 45 minutes to rise again.

Bake 15 minutes at 200°C (400°F), reduce heat to 180°C (350°F) and bake a further 45 minutes. Remove bread from tin when cool. This tastes best eaten the same day it is cooked.

Makes 1 loaf

Irish Soda Bread and Potato Yeast Bread

CARAWAY POTATO CAKES

1 cup flour (125 g)
20 g butter
4 medium potatoes, cooked and
   mashed
3 tablespoons milk
1 tablespoon caraway seeds

Place flour in a bowl and rub in butter until it resembles fine breadcrumbs. Add mashed potatoes and milk and mix to a soft dough. Turn out onto a floured board and knead until smooth.

Roll dough in a circle approximately 2.5 cm thick. With a floured biscuit cutter, cut dough into rounds. Brush with a little milk and sprinkle with caraway seeds. Bake at 180°C (350°F) for 30 minutes.

Serve with strips of cooked bacon or as an accompaniment to roasts. Alternatively, serve with Savoury Sauce (see *recipe*).

Serves 6

TASTY VARIATION:
☐ Replace caraway seeds with 1 tablespoon desiccated coconut.

1. Place flour in bowl and rub in butter.

SAVOURY SAUCE

1 tablespoon oil
1 onion, sliced
250 g minced meat
2 tomatoes, chopped
1 clove garlic, crushed
1 tablespoon chopped fresh parsley

Heat oil, add onion and fry until transparent. Add meat and stir until browned. Add tomatoes and garlic, simmering for 20 minutes (or microwave on HIGH 10 minutes, stirring once). Add parsley and serve.

Makes 1 cup (250 mL)

WARTIME VIT C
During the American Civil War, women packed potatoes in barrels filled with brine and sent them to the prisons and the front lines. By eating the potatoes with the skins on, soldiers were able to get the Vitamin C they needed.

2. Turn mixture onto floured board and knead until smooth.

3. Cut dough into rounds with biscuit cutter.

4. Brush with milk and sprinkle with caraway seeds.

5. Serve with strips of cooked bacon or savoury sauce.

ORANGE DELIGHT

125 g butter
½ cup sugar (125 g)
grated rind 1 orange
½ cup orange juice
2 eggs, lightly beaten
1½ cups self-raising flour (185 g)
1 medium potato, peeled and grated

ICING
1 cup icing sugar mixture (175 g)
orange juice
1 teaspoon butter
lemon and orange , to decorate

Cream butter and sugar until white and creamy. Add orange rind, orange juice, eggs and flour. Squeeze potato dry and add to mixture. Stir well to combine. Spoon into a greased and lined 17 cm round cake tin. Bake at 180°C (350°F) for 30 minutes. Test with skewer. It should come out clean when cake is cooked. Place a cake rack on top of loaf tin. Turn cake upside-down so cake rests on rack. Remove tin and cool before icing.

To make icing, put icing sugar into a small pan and add sufficient orange juice to make a firm mixture. Beat in butter, heat on low very briefly (or microwave on HIGH 30 seconds) and spread over cake.

POTATO CRACKERS

100 g rolled oats
100 g flour
80 g butter
2 medium potatoes, cooked and
  mashed

Combine oats and flour in a bowl. Rub in butter with fingertips, then knead in mashed potatoes to form a stiff dough.

Carefully roll out on a floured board, and cut out thin rounds using a biscuit cutter or upturned glass.

Cook on greased trays at 180°C (350°F) for 20 minutes or until biscuits are crisp and lightly browned.

Makes 20

CHOCOLATE CAKE

185 g butter
½ cup sugar (125 g)
½ teaspoon vanilla
2 eggs, beaten
½ teaspoon ground cinnamon
¼ teaspoon ground nutmeg
1½ cups self-raising flour (185 g)
½ cup milk (125 mL)
1 medium potato, peeled and grated
90 g dark chocolate, grated
½ cup hazelnuts, chopped (90 g)

ICING 1
1 egg white, whisked
1 cup icing sugar (175 g)
1 teaspoon cocoa
1 teaspoon water
grated dark chocolate, to sprinkle

ICING 2
125 g butter
1½ cups icing sugar (235 g)
1 tablespoon cocoa
2 tablespoons milk
grated dark chocolate, to sprinkle

To make cake, cream butter and sugar together until smooth. Add vanilla, eggs, spices, half the flour and half the milk. Stir well and mix in remaining flour and milk. Squeeze potato dry and stir into mixture with grated chocolate and hazelnuts.

Spoon mixture into a greased and lined loaf tin. Bake at 180°C (350°F) for 1 hour. Test with skewer to see if cake is done. It should come out clean when cake is cooked.

Place a cake rack on top of loaf tin, turn upside-down so cake rests on rack. Remove tin and cool thoroughly before icing.

If you choose to make Icing 1, combine stiffly beaten egg white, icing sugar, cocoa and water. Mix well and spread over cooled cake top. Garnish with grated chocolate.

If you choose to make Icing 2, cream butter until light and creamy. Add icing sugar, cocoa and milk. Beat well and spread over cake top. Garnish with grated chocolate.

POTATO ROLLS

1 medium potato, peeled and boiled
3 tablespoons sugar
125 g butter
2 eggs, beaten
2 cups flour (250 g)
30 g yeast

Drain potato, reserving 1 cup of potato water (250 mL). Mash potato with sugar, butter, eggs and flour. Pour reserved cup of warm potato water in a bowl and stir in yeast until dissolved. Make a well in the centre of the mixture and pour in yeast and water. Mix well.

Turn out onto a floured board and knead for 10 minutes, adding extra plain flour if necessary to make a stiff dough. Place back in bowl, cover with a damp cloth and stand in a draught-free, warm place until dough doubles in size.

Turn out again onto a floured board. Punch down and knead a further 10 minutes. Cut into 16 balls. Arrange balls on a greased tray, stand in a warm place, covered, until balls double in size. Bake at 180°C (350°F) for 20–25 minutes. Serve as dinner or barbecue rolls.

Makes 16 balls

VINCENT VAN GOGH
. . . surely must have been a potatoholic. Several of his masterpieces feature the potato, the most famous being 'The Potato Eaters' painted in 1885. His paintings often show French peasants cultivating or peeling potatoes.

Orange Delight and Chocolate Cake

Sweet Potatoes

Although botanically quite distinct, sweet potatoes have been included in our book because they are extremely popular. Traditionally associated with Creole cooking, they can be used to make delicious sweet pies, fruit salads, baked dishes and accompaniments.

INDONESIAN FRUIT AND VEGETABLE SALAD

Use a variety of fruits and vegetables in season such as:
fresh pineapple
granny-smith apples
oranges
grapefruit
firm mango
waltham grapes
cucumber
sweet potato
radishes
celery
shallots

SALAD DRESSING
2 tablespoons castor sugar
½ teaspoon salt
1 tablespoon sweet vinegar
1 tablespoon vegetable oil

Peel fruits and vegetables and slice into bite-size pieces.

Arrange on large platter attractively or put into individual dishes.

Serve with dressing in a separate bowl. Mix all ingredients together in a bowl.

COOKING SWEET POTATOES
To cook sweet potatoes, boil for 20 minutes or until tender. (Alternatively, microwave on HIGH 6 minutes per 500 g.)
Don't try peeling sweet potatoes, before cooking them. Cook potatoes and then the skins can be easily removed.

SWEET POTATO PIE

PASTRY
2 cups flour (250 g)
1 tablespoon custard powder
1 tablespoon icing sugar
175 g butter
1–2 tablespoons water
1 teaspoon lemon juice

FILLING
500 g sweet potatoes, cooked and mashed
1 cup milk (250 mL)
2 eggs, beaten
½ cup brown sugar (85 g)
1 teaspoon cinnamon
½ teaspoon nutmeg
1 tablespoon melted butter

To make the pastry, sift flour, custard powder and icing sugar into a bowl. Using fingertips, mix in butter until mixture resembles fine breadcrumbs. Using a knife cut in water and lemon juice to make a firm dough and add more water if necessary.

Turn out on to a floured board, knead lightly and roll pastry out to the size of a 20 cm pie dish. Carefully lift pastry into greased pie dish and refrigerate until required.

To make filling, combine all filling ingredients and beat until smooth. Spoon into pie shell. When pouring, hold a large spoon over the centre and allow filling to 'spill' over the spoon into the shell. This prevents pastry being weakened in the centre.

Bake at 180°C (350°F) for ½ hour or until set. Serve with ice cream or whipped cream.

Serves 6.

TASTY VARIATIONS:
☐ For filling, replace milk with 300 mL cream or sour cream;
☐ add 2 apples, peeled, cored, cooked and mashed, to potatoes.

Sweet Potato Pie

SWEET POTATO SALAD

1 kg sweet potatoes, peeled and diced
500 g potatoes, peeled and diced
20 g butter
2 onions, sliced
2 rashers bacon, diced
2 hardboiled eggs, shelled and sliced
½ cup French dressing (125 mL) (see recipe)
½ cup sour cream (125 mL)

Combine both types of potato and boil for 20 minutes or until tender (or cover sweet potatoes with microwave wrap and cook on HIGH 3 minutes, then cover potatoes with microwave wrap and 1 teaspoon water and cook on HIGH 5 minutes. Combine).

Melt butter, add onions and fry until tender. Add bacon and fry until crisp (or microwave butter, onion and bacon on HIGH 3 minutes).

Arrange potatoes, onions, bacon and eggs in a salad bowl. Combine French dressing and sour cream, and pour over salad. Chill thoroughly. Serve with lettuce and tomatoes.

Serves 6

TASTY VARIATIONS:
☐ Add 1 green apple, cored and diced;
☐ 1 tablespoon walnuts, chopped.

Sweet Potato Salad

SWEET POTATOES WITH APPLES

This dish goes well with roast or fried pork or ham.

2 cups honey (310 g)
80 g butter
4 red apples, cored and sliced into rings
750 g sweet potatoes, cooked, peeled and dry mashed
juice 2 oranges

In a pan heat together half the honey and half the butter (or microwave on HIGH 1 minute). Add sliced apples and cook for 3 minutes on each side (or microwave on HIGH 3 minutes).

Add orange juice, remaining butter and honey to potatoes, and mix well. Spoon potato on to six plates and top with cooked apples.

Serves 6

TASTY VARIATIONS:
☐ 4 tablespoons pecan nuts
☐ 6 slices pineapple

BAKED SWEET POTATO

6 sweet potatoes, peeled and cut in half
oil

Arrange potatoes in an oiled baking dish and brush lightly with oil. Bake at 180°C (350°F) for 40 minutes (see *Note*).

Serves 6

Note: To bake quickly, parboil for 20 minutes (or microwave on HIGH, allowing 6 minutes per 500 g. Stand 1 minute). Finish in oven 20 minutes.

TASTY VARIATION:
☐ For roasted potatoes, arrange potatoes on a rack and dry bake without oil.

JAMAICAN CASSEROLE

This makes a delicious accompaniment to roasts, grills and barbecued meats.

500 g sweet potatoes
40 g butter
220 g canned crushed pineapple, drained
2 tablespoons sherry or rum
½ teaspoon nutmeg
½ teaspoon cinnamon

Mash potatoes with butter. Stir in pineapple, sherry and spices. Spoon into a greased casserole and bake at 180°C (350°F) for 15 minutes (or microwave on MEDIUM 5 minutes).

Serves 6

SWEET POTATOES AU GRATIN

40 g butter
1 tablespoon flour
1 cup milk (250 mL)
750 g sweet potatoes, cooked, peeled and diced
2 teaspoons cinnamon

Melt butter, stir in flour and cook for 1 minute. Remove from heat, stir in milk, return to heat, stir until mixture boils then remove. (Alternatively, microwave butter on HIGH 1 minute then add flour and cook on HIGH 1 minute. Stir in milk and cook on HIGH 2 minutes, stir well.)

Arrange potatoes in a greased shallow casserole dish. Top with sauce. sprinkle over cinnamon then serve immediately with grills.

Serves 6

TASTY VARIATIONS:
☐ Replace cinnamon with 1 teaspoon ground cloves;
☐ before serving, sprinkle 2 tablespoons grated cheese over top and brown under griller (or microwave on HIGH until cheese bubbles).

SWEET POTATO LAYER

500 g sweet potatoes, peeled and sliced
2 onions, sliced
3 tomatoes, sliced
1 tablespoon chopped fresh basil
2 chicken stock cubes
2 cups water (500 mL)
1 cup grated tasty cheese (125 g)

Layer half the potatoes on the base of a greased casserole dish. Next, layer onions, tomatoes and basil and top with remaining potatoes. Crumble stock cubes and mix with the water. Pour over the casserole. Top with grated cheese. Bake at 180°C (350°F) for 1 hour (or microwave on HIGH 5 minutes, then MEDIUM 10 minutes). Serve warm as a complete dish.

Serves 6

TASTY VARIATIONS:
☐ To the tomato/onion layer add 1 carrot, scraped and sliced;
☐ add 500 g minced beef or lamb cooked to onion/tomato layer.

SWEET POTATO RING

1 kg sweet potatoes, cooked and peeled
3 eggs, separated
2 tablespoons melted butter
1 teaspoon ground ginger

TOPPING
4 slices stale bread, crusts removed and blended into breadcrumbs
2 tablespoons brown sugar
2 teaspoons cinnamon
2 tablespoons pecan nuts

Mash potatoes with egg yolks, butter and ginger. Whisk egg whites until stiff and fold into mixture. Grease a ring tin and spoon in mixture (or place in a microwave-safe dish).

Combine topping ingredients. Sprinkle over potato mixture and bake at 180°C (350°F) for 20 minutes (or microwave on HIGH 5 minutes). Delicious with roasts or grills.

Serves 6

TASTY VARIATIONS:
☐ Add 4 tablespoons mixed vegetables, cooked to mashed potato and serve as a complete meal;
☐ replace butter with 1 tablespoon orange juice and 1 tablespoon pineapple juice.

CANDIED SWEET POTATOES

500 g sweet potatoes, cooked and peeled
60 g butter
1 cup brown sugar (180 g)

Arrange potatoes in a greased baking dish. Melt butter and sugar together and pour over potatoes. Bake at 180°C (350°F) for 20 minutes, basting occasionally.

(Alternatively, melt butter and sugar together on HIGH 2 minutes. Pour mixture over potatoes, microwave on HIGH 3 minutes.) Serve with roasts.

Serves 6

Sweet Potatoes au Gratin

Children's Special Spuds

Appetising though the potato undoubtedly is, every parent sometimes has trouble enticing their children to eat good food. The following recipes are designed especially to appeal to children, visually and tastewise.

EGGS IN CARS

2 large potatoes, peeled
4 hardboiled eggs, shelled
8 sultanas
16 small cherry tomatoes
2 slices cucumber
1 carrot, grated
1 cup peas, cooked (200 g)
1 cup grated cheese (125 g)

Boil potatoes for 20 minutes or until tender (or microwave on HIGH for 6–8 minutes). Cut each potato in half lengthways. Place potato half cut-side down on a plate. Scoop out a hole large enough to support egg, approximately 2 cm deep. Using a sharp knife, pierce 2 small holes in egg for eyes, insert sultanas. Sit egg in potato.

Arrange two tomatoes as wheels on each side of potato half. Cut cucumber slices in half. Using a sharp knife make a small slit in potato in front of egg, insert half cucumber slice, cut side down. Arrange grated carrot, as hair, on top of egg. Arrange 2 rows of peas as road, in front and behind car, placing grated cheese in between rows of peas. Repeat with remaining ingredients.

Makes 4

SPUD'S FUNNY FACE

1 large potato, baked or boiled
with skin on
1 raw carrot, scraped and washed
1 tablespoon cooked peas
alfalfa, to garnish

Cut a small slice from both ends of the potato. Cut off about 1 cm of the carrot's pointed end. Grate remaining carrot. Sit the potato on its end on a plate.

Carefully make two small holes for eyes and place a pea in each. Make a hole for the nose and push in the flat carrot end. Make a slit for the mouth and fill with a strip of carrot. Pile grated carrot on top for hair. Surround potato with alfalfa. Heat in the oven at 180°C (350°F) for 10 minutes (or microwave on HIGH 1–2 minutes).

Serves 1

Eggs in Cars, Spud's Funny Face, Oven Baked Chips, and Funny/Sad Potato Face

FUNNY/SAD POTATO FACE

4 potatoes, peeled
1 tablespoon butter
2 tablespoons milk
1 egg
8 slices cucumber
4 tear drop tomatoes
4 cherry tomatoes
4 cocktail frankfurts, cooked
8 lettuce leaves
alfalfa, to garnish

Chop potatoes and boil in water for 20 minutes or until tender (microwave in a freezer bag on HIGH for 10–12 minutes). Add butter, milk and egg and mash until smooth.

To make funny face spread ¼ of potato mixture on the base of a dinner plate. Use 2 cucumber slices for eyes. Use tear drop tomato for nose, cut a cherry tomato in half and place with cut sides down as cheeks. Cut a frankfurt in half lengthways and place with curve upwards for a smiling mouth or curve downwards for a sad mouth. Make hair with two lettuce leaves and alfalfa sprouts. Repeat with remaining ingredients.

Makes 4

OVEN-BAKED CHIPS

2 medium potatoes, peeled and washed
2 tablespoons oil

Cut potatoes into chips and pat dry with kitchen paper towels. Arrange chips on oiled oven tray. Sprinkle with oil and bake at 250°C (475°F) for 30 minutes, turning chips once.

Serves 2

Bubble and Squeak

Last but by no means least, there are leftovers. So potentially useful, so irritatingly wasteful when you have to throw them away.

LEFTOVER SOUP

310 g canned red kidney beans, drained
1 medium potato, peeled and diced
1 onion, diced
1 carrot, scraped and diced
1 zucchini, diced
1 stalk celery, diced
440 g canned tomatoes, liquid reserved
1 chicken stock cube
water

Rinse kidney beans in cold water. Place in a pan with all vegetables, stock cube and sufficient water to cover. Bring to the boil, lower heat and simmer 1 hour. Serve in individual bowls with toast.

Serves 6

HOMEMADE SAUSAGES

250 g cooked meat or chicken, finely minced or diced
20 g butter, melted
2 shallots, finely chopped
1 tablespoon chopped fresh parsley
2 tablespoons water
1 beef or chicken stock cube
1 teaspoon flour
2 eggs, beaten
4 medium potatoes, cooked and mashed with 40 g butter
oil, for shallow-frying

Combine meat, butter, shallots, parsley, water and stock cube in a pan. Bring to the boil, then lower heat and simmer until water evaporates. Remove from heat and stir in flour and eggs. Mix well, return to heat and stir until thickened. Mix in mashed potatoes.

Spoon mixture into a greased casserole dish and refrigerate overnight. Next day, turn out onto a floured board and roll spoonfuls of mixture into tiny sausage shapes.

Heat oil and fry sausages both sides until crisp and brown. Serve as nibbles with a barbecue.

Serves 6

BUBBLE AND SQUEAK

A traditional favourite — the unusual name comes from the noise it makes in a pan while cooking!

2 rashers bacon
1 onion, sliced
1 medium potato, cooked and mashed
¼ cabbage, shredded and lightly steamed

Cook bacon rashers then remove with a slotted spoon. Add onions to pan and gently fry until tender. Add potato and cabbage. Press together to form a large cake. Cook until underneath is brown. Turn with a spatula and brown on other side. Serve on toast or with eggs.

Serves 6

PATTA CAKE

The name refers to patting the mixture between the palms of the hands to form a flat cake.

4 medium potatoes, cooked and mashed
2 tablespoons milk
1 tablespoon self-raising flour
250 g cooked, minced meat
oil, for shallow-frying

Mash potatoes with milk. Add self-raising flour, and mix to a stiff dough, adding more milk if necessary. Divide mix into six portions.

Press one portion out with your hand to make a circle. Fill with a spoonful of meat, fold and press edges closed. Gently press in palms till flattened. Repeat with remaining meat and potato mixture.

Heat oil and fry cakes until lightly browned on both sides. Serve with bacon or green salad.

Serves 6

Patta Cake and Leftover Soup

How to Grow Your Own

Potatoes

The potato or Irish potato (*Solanum tuberosum*) originated in the temperate regions of the Andes in South America where it has been used by the native people as food for some 2000 years.

The potato plant is a perennial herb with straggling, semi-erect branches bearing leaves with three or four pairs of oval-shaped leaflets. The flowers are white or purplish and develop into a small, green tomato-like berry. The plant has fibrous roots and many rhizomes or underground stems which become swollen at the tip to form the edible tubers. The tubers are also used for planting and are commonly referred to as 'seed potatoes'.

Potatoes are a very adaptable crop but prefer temperate or cool climates. However, the plants are extremely susceptible to frost. In warm regions, potatoes can be planted at almost any time of the year, but early autumn, winter or early spring planting are recommended. In temperate climates an early crop can be planted in spring and a late crop planted in midsummer. In cold climates, plantings are made in late spring or midsummer only so that the plants are fully grown before cold weather arrives.

Potatoes are adaptable to both light and heavy soils but good drainage is essential. Prepare the bed to spade depth well before planting so that the soil is in friable condition for the tubers to expand evenly.

Tubers for planting should be 30–60 g in weight but large tubers can be cut into blocky pieces provided there is at least one 'eye' or sprout on each piece. Always buy government-certified seed potatoes which are harvested from crops free of virus and other diseases. Certified seed potatoes are available from plant nurseries and garden stores in late winter or early spring. Where two crops can be grown in one year save some tubers from the most

Digging potatoes

90

productive plants in the early crop for later planting.

Before planting, spread the tubers or cut pieces in a shady spot for a week or two. This "greening" or "chitting" hardens the sprouts which are less liable to damage. Discard any tubers which develop spindly shoots or other blemishes. A plastic bag (2 – 3 kg) of certified seed potatoes contains enough tubers for 40 to 60 plants. If the crop is well grown, this should provide enough potatoes for the average family.

Make the planting furrows about 15 cm deep and space them 60 – 75 cm apart. Sprinkle pre-planting fertiliser along the bottom and cover with 5 cm of soil from the sides. Set the tubers or pieces of tubers on the soil layer in the furrow about 30 cm apart, then fill in with the remaining soil and rake the bed level. Potato plants will break the surface in about three weeks.

Cultivate between the rows to destroy weeds and gradually hill soil against the plants as they grow. This supports the sprawling stems and prevents greening of tubers formed close to the surface. Additional fertiliser is seldom necessary but the plants must be watered regularly to promote smooth, well-developed tubers.

Potatoes are ready for digging in 16 to 20 weeks from planting. For "new" potatoes, you can start digging when the lower leaves turn yellow – usually about three weeks after the plants have flowered. Potatoes for storage should not be lifted until the plants have died off completely. After removing the soil from the potatoes, discard any showing skin damage or blemishes and store in a cool, airy place which must also be dark to prevent greening. Wooden boxes and cardboard cartons from which light is excluded or thick hessian sacks are good containers for storage.

Diseases and pests
Early blight (target soil) and late blight (Irish blight) cause leaf spotting and can seriously damage plants and reduce yields. Several virus diseases (leafroll, spotted wilt and purple top or big bud) attack potato plants. Always use certified seed potatoes or those saved from disease-free plants. Most virus diseases are transmitted by aphids, thirps or jassids so regular sprays of recommended chemicals will control these sap-sucking insects and help to prevent virus transmission. Infected plants should be removed and burned.

Potato moth is the worst insect pest of potatoes. The small caterpillars of the moth will attack both leaves and tubers. If the plants are hilled with soil as they grow, infestation of the tubers is unlikely.

Sweet Potatoes

The sweet potato (*Ipomoea batatas*) is thought to have originated in South America but was also recorded by early explorers in the East Indies and the Philippine Islands. The plants are perennials with trailing vines bearing a dense mass of arrow-shaped leaves. The edible, underground tubers may be creamy-white, buff, brown, pink or purple in colour. The flesh is usually white but some cultivars have yellow or pink flesh. The sweet potato is a major crop in countries with warm temperate, subtropical or tropical climates and the cooked tubers are especially valued as high-energy foods because of their starch and sugar content.

Sweet potatoes are sometimes called yams. The yam (*Dioscorea batatas*) is also a perennial vine with edible tubers which may reach 60 – 100 cm in length. The cultivation of yams is confined to some tropical countries and the islands of the Pacific Ocean.

As the sweet potato is a warm season plant, it is susceptible to frost, and requires a growing season of about six months. Its cultivation is not recommended in cool temperate or cold regions. In the home garden, the rambling vines need a lot of space to grow.

Light soils or those enriched with organic matter to provide a friable, crumb structure are most suitable. The soil is prepared in much the same way as for potatoes. Sweet potato plants are started from shoots or cuttings from tubers. Unlike potatoes, which are stem tubers with a number of "eyes", sweet potatoes are root tubers which produce new shoots at the top of the tuber in the same way as dahlias. Shoots or cuttings may be available in late winter or early spring from plant nurseries. Alternatively, tubers can be purchased and buried in a box of moist sand. If kept in a warm spot, shoots will soon develop. When the shoots are 10 – 15 cm long, carefully separate them from the parent tuber for transplanting.

After spreading a pre-planting fertiliser along the line where the plants are to grow, rake it into the topsoil and form a ridge about 10 cm above the garden bed for planting the shoots. Space the shoots about 30 cm apart and allow 60 – 75 cm between rows. For the average family 20 to 24 plants should be sufficient.

Cultivate between plants and rows to control weeds until the vines cover the soil in between. Water the vines regularly and lift them up occasionally to prevent roots developing at the nodes (joints) of the vines. New plants formed at the nodes tend to restrict tuber development under the parent plant. Additional fertiliser is rarely necessary if a pre-planting fertiliser has been used.

Tubers should not be dug until the plants are yellow and die back. Tuber quality improves with maturity but if cold weather or frost is expected, dig the tubers immediately. Tubers subjected to low temperatures (10°C or less) are damaged and will not store well. After digging, leave the vines and tubers in heaps with hessian sacks or plastic at night to avoid low temperature damage. Mature tubers have a firm skin and, when cut with a knife, the surface dries quickly and cleanly. If the tubers are not mature, a milky sap exudes from the cut surface which discolours to a dark green on drying. Before storing, discard any tubers with blemishes or symptoms of rotting. Store them in a warm, dry place; the storage temperature must not fall below 10°C.

Diseases and pests
Sweet potatoes are remarkably free of diseases and pests. Control leaf-eating caterpillars with sprays recommended by your local agriculture department. The mass of dense foliage must be sprayed thoroughly.

GLOSSARY

INGREDIENTS

BACON RASHERS: bacon slices.

BEEF

Mince: ground beef.
Blade: cut of beef next to the shoulder blade, ideal for hot pots and casseroles.
Chuck: cut of beef taken from between the neck and shoulder blade, ideal for hot pots and casseroles.
Fillet steak: piece taken from the underside of the rump and sirloin, which has little fat.
Rump steak: cut of beef taken from the hinder part of the animal behind the loin.
Scotch fillet: also called ribeye; cut of beef with some of the best muscle meat, taken from near the ribs. It can be roasted in one piece or cut into steaks.

BICARBONATE OF SODA: baking soda, an ingredient in baking powder.

BREADCRUMBS

Soft: fresh breadcrumbs, made with one or two day old bread in a blender or food processor.
Dry: commercial packaged breadcrumbs.

BURGHUL: hulled wheat, available at supermarkets, delicatessens and health food stores. It is also known as 'bulkar' (Arabic), 'pourgouri' (Greek) and 'bular' (Turkish).

BUTTER: use salted butter unless otherwise specified.

CABBAGE: use green cabbage (also known as roundhead or common cabbage) unless otherwise specified e.g. red cabbage or white cabbage.

CALAMARI: squid. Prepare as directed according to a particular recipe.

CAPSICUM: sweet peppers, red and green.

CHEESE

Munster: substitute Brie if Munster is unavailable.
Tasty: use mature Cheddar.

CHICKEN: recipes specify exact weight required e.g. 1.2 kg.

CHILLI: use fresh chillies where specified, with great care. Rubber gloves can protect the skin from burning but make sure you never touch your eyes while preparing chilli. As the seeds are the hottest part, these can be removed and discarded if preferred.

COPHA: a form of purified coconut oil, also sold as coconut butter, Copha Butter and Kremelta (registered trademarks).

COCONUT, DESICCATED: shredded coconut.

CORNFLOUR: cornstarch.

CREAM: also known as single, light or coffee cream.
Thickened cream: double, heavy or whipping cream.
Sour cream: soured or dairy sour cream. Also available in a fat-reduced form which has fewer calories.

EGGPLANT: aubergine.

ESSENCE: extract.

FLOUR: use plain or all-purpose flour unless otherwise stated.
Self-raising flour: all-purpose flour to which baking powder has been added in the proportions of 1 cup (125 g) flour: 2 teaspoons (10 grams) baking powder.

FRUIT: we specify fresh or canned (tinned), but if no fresh fruit is available, you can substitute canned. The dish may taste slightly different.

GHEE: Indian clarified buffalo-milk butter. Can be bought at large supermarkets and delicatessens.

GINGER

Fresh ginger root: available at a green grocer's or fruiterer's; usually peeled and chopped before using.
Powdered ginger: ground ginger, available in spice jars.

GOLDEN SYRUP: maple or pancake syrup can be used instead.

HERBS: our recipes specify whether to use fresh or dried herbs, but if you need to replace fresh herbs with dried, the ratio is 1:4 — 1 teaspoon of dried to 4 teaspoons (1 tablespoon) of fresh herbs.

LAMB

Chump chops: chops cut from the chump section located between the leg and the loin.
Cutlets: chops cut from the rib loin; can be grilled, fried or roasted.
Leg chops: chops taken from the top of the leg.
Loin chops: standard cut of lamb, veal or pork, cut from the upper flank and including the lower ribs.
Rack of lamb: cutlets from rib loin section still joined together.
Shanks: pieces cut from the top part of the legs.

MIXED SPICE: finely ground spice combination, including allspice, nutmeg and cinnamon; used to flavour cakes and buns.

MUESLI: granola.

MUSHROOMS, DRIED: available from supermarkets and delicatessens, they need to be soaked for 20 minutes before using.

OIL: use a vegetable or olive oil, unless otherwise specified.

PARISIAN ESSENCE: flavouring extract available in supermarkets and delicatessens. Can be replaced with Hansell's Gravy Browner (registered trademark).

PAPPADUMS: thin crisp Indian wafer bread made from spiced potato or rice flour. They are best cooked by frying in oil but can also be grilled.

PAW PAW: papaya or papaw.

PIMENTO: allspice.

PIMIENTO: canned or bottled type of chilli pepper.

PORK

Butterfly chop or steak: boned, rind removed loin chop or steak, split in half and opened out.

Fillet: boned, rind removed piece cut from the underside of the rump and sirloin.

Medallions: rind removed, boned, round pieces taken from the loin.

Spareribs: meat cut from the ribs still containing rib bones.

Steaks: pieces cut from the leg or rump across the grain of the muscle.

Tenderloin: a very tender strip of meat, part of the loin under the ribs.

PRAWN: shrimp.

PROSCIUTTO HAM: a fine quality cured ham from Italy. The ham is rubbed with salt, sugar, nitrates, pepper, allspice, nutmeg, coriander and mustard. It is then packed for 10 days when the process is repeated. Upon maturing, the ham is pressed, steamed and rubbed with pepper. Local tradition maintains that the hams get their flavour by prolonged aging in the mountain air.

PUMPKIN: use any type.

ROCK MELON: also known as ogen melon and cantaloupe.

SAUCES

Hoisin sauce: Chinese sauce made from onions, garlic and salted black beans.

Soy sauce: made from soya beans; a great variety is available, especially from Asian foodstores. Experiment to find which one you prefer to use with different foods.

SHALLOTS: very small white onions also known as scallions and spring onions.

Spring onions: larger, white-bulbed sweet onions.

STOCK CUBE: bouillon cube; can be replaced with 1 teaspoon powdered stock or bouillon.

SUGAR

Use any sugar you prefer unless otherwise specified. The most common types are the following:

Caster: fine white granulated sugar.

Raw: brown granulated sugar.

Brown: soft, moist sugar.

Icing: confectioner's or powdered sugar.

SULTANAS: seedless white raisins.

TAHINA: a paste made from crushed sesame seeds. It can also be bought from delicatessens and some health food shops.

TARAMA: salted fish roe. Available from supermarkets and delicatessens.

TOMATO PASTE: also known as tomato concentrate.

TOMATO SAUCE: tomato ketchup.

VEAL

Chops: taken from the loin and the ribs.

Cutlets: taken from the loin and the ribs.

Escalopes: thin slices, often coated in breadcrumbs and fried.

WHOLEMEAL: wholewheat.

YOGHURT: use natural or unflavoured yoghurt.

ZUCCHINI: courgette.

EQUIPMENT AND TERMS

CAN, CANNED: tin, tinned.

CRUSHED: minced, pressed.

FRYING PAN: skillet.

GRILL: broil.

GREASEPROOF PAPER: waxproof paper.

LAMINGTON TIN: oven tray 4 cm (1½ inches) deep. Grease and use as a biscuit or cake tin.

PAPER CASES: paper baking cases or cups; also available as petits fours (type of French small cake) cases.

PAPER TOWEL: absorbent kitchen paper towel.

PLASTIC WRAP: cling film.

PUNNET: small box or basket containing about 250 g (8 oz) of fruit.

SANDWICH TIN: layer cake pan.

SEEDED: stoned or pitted — stone removed and discarded.

SPRING-FORM CAKE TIN: spring pan or loose-bottomed cake tin.

SWISS ROLL TIN: jelly roll pan.

Oven Temperatures

	Celsius	Fahrenheit
Very slow	120	250
Slow	140-150	275-300
Moderately slow	160	325
Moderate	180	350
Moderately hot	190	375
Hot	200	400
	220	425
	230	450
Very hot	250-260	475-500

Measurements

Standard Metric Measures

1 cup	=	250 mL
1 tablespoon	=	20 mL
1 teaspoon	=	5 mL

All spoon measurements are level

Cup Measures

1 × 250 mL cup =	Grams	Ounces
breadcrumbs, dry	125	4½
soft	60	2
butter	250	8¾
cheese, grated		
cheddar	125	4½
coconut, desiccated	95	3¼
flour, cornflour	130	4¾
plain or self-raising	125	4½
wholemeal	135	4¾
fruit, mixed dried	160	5¾
honey	360	12¾
sugar, caster	225	7¾
crystalline	250	8¾
icing	175	6¾
moist brown	170	6
nuts	125	4

Freshly dug potatoes

Potatoes make a good commercial crop

Index

A
Aioli Sauce Dip   16
American Filling   74
Anna Potatoes   46
Apple
    Sauce   44
    with Sweet Potatoes   84
Arabian Mixed Vegetables   58
Avocado
    Farci   17
    and Potato Soup   63

B
Bacon
    and Mushroom Filling   73
    Sauce, Tangy   44
Baked Creamed Potatoes   55
Baked Potato Skins with Aioli
    Sauce Dip   16
Baked Potatoes   12
Baked Salmon Croquettes with
    Quick Tomato Sauce   68
Baked Sweet Potato   84
Baked Tortellini   41
Basic New Potato Salad   30
Basic Potato Salad   26
Batter   14, 69
    Beer   23, 69
Bean
    and Beef Filling, Savoury   74
    Mexican Filling   72
Beef
    and Bean Filling, Savoury   74
    Bourguignon   39
    with Potatoes and Beer   39
Beer Batter   23
Beetroot and Potato Salad with Dill
    Dressing   32
Berny Potatoes   69
Best Baked Potatoes   12
Birds Nest   60
Blue Potato Filling   74
Bread
    Irish Soda   76
    Poori   63
    Potato Rolls   81
    Potato Yeast   76
Broccoli Birds Nest   60
Bubble and Squeak   89
Burghul and Potato Balls   64

C
Cabbage Calcannon   55
Cake
    Chocolate   81
    Orange Delight   81
Calcannon   55
Candied Sweet Potato   85
Caraway Potato Cakes   78
Carrot
    and Potato Casserole   55
    Soup   62
Castle, Potato   55
Cauliflower Soup   40

Celeriac Filling   74
Champ   52
Cheese
    and Apple Filling, Crunchy   74
    Blue Potato Filling   74
    and Chutney Filling   74
    and Potato Fritters   58
    Sauce   55, 59
Cheese Croquettes with Mustard
    Sauce   68
Cheesy Potato Fans   48
Chicken
    and Almond Filling   72
    Roast   70
    Salad   28
    with Sauteed Potatoes and
        Mushrooms   43
Chips
    Oven-Baked   86
    Perfect   66
Chocolate Cake   81
Choux Potatoes   49
Classic Dressing   33
Corn
    and Potato Puffs   69
    and Potato Soup   40
Cornish Pasties   38
Crab Mornay   22
Crackers, Potato   81
Creamy Salad Dressing   32
Creamy Scallop Soup   22
Crepes, Luscious Potato   34
Crispy Potatoes   69
Croquettes
    Baked Salmon, with Quick
        Tomato Sauce   68
    Cheese, with Mustard
        Sauce   68
Crunchy Cheese and Apple
    Filling   74
Cucumber
    Dip   14
    and Lime Soup   19
Cups, Potato   13
Curried
    Egg Filling   74
    Meat Balls   39
    Potato   56
    Potato Salad   28
    Potato Soup   18

D
Dahin Aloo   63
Dauphinoise Potatoes   50
Deep-Fried Vegetables with
    Tomato Dip   14
Dill
    Dressing   32
    Mustard Potato Salad   24
Dip
    Aioli Sauce   16
    Cucumber   14
    Dahin Aloo   63
    Tomato   14
Doloise Salad   32
Dosa with Potato Stuffing   63

Dressing   82
    see also Mayonnaise
    Classic   33
    Creamy   32
    Dill   32
    French   29
    Herb   33
    Tomato   33
    Vinaigrette   29
Dry Roasted Potatoes   48
Duchesse Potatoes   46
Dumplings, Potato   52

E
Eggplant and Potato Bake   63
Eggs
    see also Omelette
    in Cars   87
    Filling, Curried   74

F
Festive Potato Salad   28
Fettuccine
    with Potato and Tomato
        Sauce   16
    with Potatoes and
        Silverbeet   41
Filling
    American   74
    Bacon and Mushroom   73
    Blue Potato   74
    Celeriac   74
    Cheese and Chutney   74
    Chicken and Almond   72
    Crunchy Cheese and
        Apple   74
    Curried Egg   74
    Healthy   13
    Mexican   72
    Mushroom   72
    Prawn   73
    Savoury Beef and Bean   74
    Seafood   74
    Sour Cream and Shallot   73
    Tomato and Prawn   74
    Vegetarian   73
Finnish Pie   44
Fish
    see also Salmon
    Fisherman's Pie   36
    a la Greque   43
    Parcels   42
    Smoked Fish Cakes with Tartare
        Sauce   68
Fisherman's Pie   36
Flan
    Cheesy Potato   48
    Pastry   38
    Potato   39
Flapjacks, Potato   58
French Dressing   29
French Potato Balls   49
French Vegetable Salad   31
Fried Potato Skins with Aioli Sauce
    Dip   16

Fritters, Cheese and Potato   58
Fruit and Vegetable Salad,
    Indonesian   82
Fruity Stuffing   70
Funny Face   86
Funny/Sad Potato Face   87

G
Galette, Potato   76
Garlic
    Aioli Sauce   16
    Mashed Potatoes   54
    Sauce   23
Gnocchi
    with Cheese Sauce   59
    Semolina, with Veal and Tomato
        Sauce   42
Golden Nugget Soup   62
Greek Salad   30
Green Herb Soup   18

H
Ham and Potato Scones   55
Hash Browns   52
Healthy Filling   13
Herb
    Dressing   33
    Potatoes   12
    Soup, Green   18
    Stuffing for Chicken   70
Herring Potato Salad   32
Homemade Sausages   88
Honeyed Roast Potatoes   48
Hot Potato Salad   30
Huancaina Papas   32

I
Idaho Jacket Potatoes   12
Indonesian Fruit and Vegetable
    Salad   82
Irish Soda Bread   76
Italian Potato Salad   28

J
Jacket Potatoes, Idaho   12
Jamaican Casserole   84
Janssons Temptation   28

K
Kugel, Potato   52

L
Lamb Navarin with New
    Potatoes   39
Leek Soup (Vichyssoise)   22
Leftover Soup   89
Luscious Potato Crepes   34
Lyonnaise Potatoes   46

M

Mashed Potatoes, Garlic 54
Mayonnaise
    Pesto 24
    Spicy 26
    Tasty 29
Meat Balls, Curried 39
Meat Loaf with Tasty Tomato
    Topping 42
Mexican Filling 72
Minestrone 40
Mock Whitebait 69
Mushroom
    and Bacon Filling 73
    Filling 72
    Pie, Finnish 44
Mustard Sauce 68

N

Nicoise Salad 28
Noisettes 69
Nomad Potatoes 52
Nut and Potato Salad 31

O

Omelette
    with Crispy Pan-Fried
      Potatoes 44
    Potato 34
    Spanish 52
Onion Stuffing 70
Orange Delight 81
Oven-Baked Chips 86

P

Pancakes
    see also Crepes; Flapjacks
    Potato, with Sour Cream and
      Apple Sauce 44
Parathas 64
Pasta see Fettuccine; Gnocchi;
    Tortellini
Pasties
    Cornish 38
    Dosa with Potato Stuffing 63
    Parathas 64
Pastry, Flan 38
Patta Cake 89
Peanut Sauce, Spicy 64
Perfect Chips 66
Peruvian Balls in Spicy Peanut
    Sauce 64
Pesto Mayonnaise 24
Pie
    Finnish 44
    Fisherman's 36
    Sweet Potato 82
    Vegetarian 59
Pommes de Terre Berny 69
Pommes Noisettes 69
Poori 63
Potato
    Anna 46
    and Avocado Soup 63
    with Beef'n'Beer 39
    and Beetroot Salad with Dill
      Dressing 32
    Castle 55

Crackers 81
Cups 13
Curry 56
Dumplings 52
Flan 39
Flapjacks 58
Galette 76
Kugel 52
Nut Salad 31
Omelette 34
Pancakes with Sour Cream and
    Apple Sauce 44
Rolls 81
Romanoff 46
Sambal 63
Scallops 69
and Silverbeet with
    Fettuccine 41
Smitana 49
Souffle with Tangy Bacon
    Sauce 44
Sticks 16
and Tomato Sauce 16
Yeast Bread 76
and Yoghurt 58
Potato Peel Stock 62
Potato Salad
    Basic 26
    Basic New 30
    Festive 28
    Herring 32
    Hot 30
    Italian 28
    with Pesto Mayonnaise 24
    with Spicy Mayonnaise 26
Prawns
    in Beer Batter 23
    Filling 73
    in Garlic Sauce 23
    and Tomato Filling 74
Puffs, Spicy Potato 19
Pumpkin
    Golden Nugget Soup 62

R

Roast Chicken 70
Roasted Potatoes 48
    Honeyed 48
Rolls, Potato 81
Romanoff Potatoes 46

S

Salad
    see also Potato Salad
    Chicken 28
    Curried Potato 28
    Dill-Mustard Potato 24
    Doloise 32
    French Vegetable 31
    Greek 30
    Huancaina Papas 32
    Indonesian Fruit and
      Vegetable 82
    Janssons Temptation 28
    Nicoise 28
    Seafood 31
    Sliced Potatoes Vinaigrette 26
    Sweet Potato 84

Salad Dressing see Dressing
Salmon
    Croquettes, Baked, with Quick
      Tomato Sauce 68
    Rolls 42
Sambal, Potato 63
Satay Sauce 19
Sauce
    see also Dressing
    Aioli 16
    Apple 44
    Cheese 55
    Garlic 23
    Mustard 68
    Potato and Tomato 16
    Satay 19
    Savoury 78
    Spicy Peanut 64
    Tangy Bacon 44
    Tartare 68
    Tasty Cheese 59
    Tomato 68
    Veal and Tomato 42
Sausages, Homemade 88
Sauteed Potatoes
    with Chicken and
      Mushrooms 43
    in Lemon and Garlic 49
Savoury Beef and Bean
    Filling 74
Savoury Sauce 78
Scallop Soup, Creamy 22
Scallops, Potato 69
Scampi in Garlic Sauce 23
Scones, Ham and Potato 55
Seafood
    see also Crab; Prawns; Scallop;
      Scampi
    in a Basket 20
    Filling 74
    Salad 31
Semolina Gnocchi with Veal and
    Tomato Sauce 42
Silverbeet
    Birds Nest 60
    and Potatoes with
      Fettuccine 41
Skins, Baked or Fried, with Aioli
    Sauce Dip 16
Sliced Potatoes Vinaigrette 26
Smitana Potatoes 49
Smoked Fish Cakes with Tartare
    Sauce 68
Souffle, Potato, with Tangy Bacon
    Sauce 44
Soup
    Carrot 62
    Cauliflower 40
    Corn and Potato 40
    Creamy Scallop 22
    Cucumber and Lime 19
    Curried Potato 18
    Golden Nugget 62
    Green Herb 18
    Leftover 89
    Minestrone 40
    Potato and Avocado 63
    Split Pea and Potato 40
    Tomato Cream 62
    Vichyssoise 22

Sour Cream and Shallot
    Filling 73
Spanish Omelette 52
Spicy Mayonnaise 26
Spicy Peanut Sauce 64
Spicy Potato Puffs 19
Spinach
    Birds Nest 60
    and Potato Castle 55
Split Pea and Potato Soup 40
Spud's Funny Face 86
Sticks, Potato 16
Stock, Potato Peel 62
Stuffing
    Fruity 70
    Herb, for Chicken 70
    Onion 70
Sugar-Glazed Potatoes 48
Sweet Potato
    with Apples 84
    Baked 84
    Candied 85
    au Gratin 85
    Jamaican Casserole 84
    Layer 85
    Pie 82
    Ring 85
    Salad 84

T

Tangy Bacon Sauce 44
Taramosalata 14
Tartare Sauce 68
Tasty Cheese Sauce 59
Tasty Mayonnaise 29
Tomato
    Cream Soup 62
    Dip 14
    Dressing 33
    and Potato Sauce 16
    and Prawn Filling 74
    Sauce, Quick 68
Tortellini, Baked 41

V

Veal and Tomato Sauce 42
Vegetables
    Arabian Mixed 58
    Deep-Fried, with Tomato
      Dip 14
    Salad, French 31
Vegetarian Filling 73
Vegetarian Pie 59
Vichyssoise 22
Vinaigrette 26, 29

W

Whitebait, Mock 69

Y

Yeast Bread, Potato 76
Yoghurt
    Dahin Aloo 63
    and Potatoes 58